The Haute Rou

Chamonix-Zermatt

M000215642

The Haute Route

Chamonix-Zermatt

A guide for skiers and mountain walkers

Peter Cliff

First edition 1993, reprinted 1997, 2001, fully revised 2003, reprinted 2006

Copyright © Peter Cliff 1993

This edition published by Cordee Ltd, 3a de Montfort Street, Leicester, LE1 7HD, www.cordee.co.uk

Printed by Fratellii Spada SpA, Rome

ISBN: 1 871890 21 7

A catalogue record for this book is available from the British Library

Cover photgraph supplied by Mountain Spirit
62 Grampian Road, Aviemore, Inverness-Shire, PH22 1PD
Telephone 01479 811788
Email: info@mountainspirit.co.uk

Mountain Spirit – We have tried our very best to source the cutting edge equipment available on the market so whatever your sport be it Telemark, Ski Mountaineering, Cross Country, Winter Mountaineering or Climbing be rest assured we will be stocking the very best.

Contents

On the route diagrams the ski route is shown as a solid blue line and the walking route is as a dotted blue line. Where the two routes are similar, only a solid blue line is shown and cross reference must be made between the Skiing and Walking text in order to get the full description.

Acknowledgements

From time to time I have received advice from all the guardians along the Haute Route, especially the former guardians. Willy Berra (Trient), Marc André Calox and Bernard Perret (Valsorey), Gerard Michaud (Chanrion), Elisabeth and the late Jean Vuigner (Vignettes).

The following Guides have advised on the route: Alain Cretton (Argentière), Fred Harper (Britain), Kathy Murphy (Britain), Michael Thivièrge (Chamonix) and Dave Walsh (Britain).

Of all the people who have helped most I thank the British guides Jim Kerr (research on the route between Grand St Bernard and the Velan Hut) and Malcom Creasey (for supplying material and for checking certain route descriptions and times).

All photographs are by the author with the exception of the one on page 18 which is by Fred Harper. The maps and diagrams are by Doug Godlington.

Introduction

The Haute Route was first done as a walking route in 1861 by members of the Alpine Club and they called it the High Level Road. As skiing developed it became popular as a ski mountaineering route and the French name Haute Route was used. There are now many other Haute Routes in the Alps and elsewhere, to the extent that the French tend to refer to this one as Chamonix-Zermatt. But this was the original Haute Route and when someone talks about the Haute Route, there is no doubt about which one they mean.

There are several variations, the longest and hardest being the Classic Route with the Zermatt-Saas Fee Variation, which crosses 23 glaciers and has a total ascent and descent of 10,000 metres (33,000 feet) - by comparison Mount Everest is 8848m (29,028 feet) above sea level.

Why is the Haute Route so justifiably popular? One of the reasons must be that it is a traverse, which is always particularly satisfying. In this case one starts from Chamonix, the centre of alpinism in France, passes through probably the finest high alpine scenery in the Pennine Alps, steps briefly in to Italy, and descends under the North Face of the Matterhorn to Zermatt – the centre of all the early mountain exploration in Switzerland. A second reason for its popularity is that the scenery is really unbelievable. On the first day, coming out of the Grande Montets, the view is stunning: Les Aiguilles Rouges; l'Aiguille du Chardonnet; l'Aiguille d'Argentière; le Tour Noir; Mont Dolent and l'Aiguille de Triolet. As you descend to the Argentière Glacier the view on the right progressively opens up until you are right under the huge North Faces of the Verte, Droites and Courtes.

Each of the variations has its own advantages, and the main ones are covered in this guidebook. But the ski route over the Plateau du Couloir opened up by Marcel Kurz and Prof Roget in 1911 was recognised as something special and it became known as The Classic Haute Route.

Most people will do the Haute Route for the pleasure of moving through exceptional high Alpine scenery. Demands will be made on fitness, skills and judgement; and great pleasure will be derived from resolving those problems.

Others will go for different reasons, not least Stephane Schaffter (a Geneva Guide) who in 1990 went from the summit of Mont Blanc to the summit of Monte Rosa in 36 hours. He reached the Valsorey Hut in 8 hours and had his only rest here (a meal, a shower and 20 minutes sleep).

General Points

Personal skills

Since the Haute Route is a high glacier tour, experience must exist in the following areas: weather, avalanches, crevasses, route choice, navigation, steep ground, and maybe accident procedure. In a guided party the expertise for all those areas will be in one person, the Guide. In a party without a Guide two or more members may bring different skills to the expedition, resulting in a sharing of decision-making.

In summer each person should, at the least, be a fit and competent walker, used to walking on crampons and to handling an ice axe. To do the route on skis requires the ability to maintain a steady rate of descent off-piste in varied snow conditions – a useful yardstick is strong basic (i.e. feet apart) parallel on the piste. It is best not to underestimate the skiing standard required: long days, difficult snow and a rucksack can make considerable demands – those with ski technique will cope, those without will struggle.

Conditions

It is possible to ski the route at any time in the winter, and this is when the early attempts were all made. But in January and February the days are short, the temperatures are low, the crevasse bridges are often hidden under a blanket of unstable snow, and many of the big winter snow storms are still to fall. The huts are closed, although winter rooms are always left open so shelter is available even if it means carrying your own food. A big plus for this time of year is that there will not be many other people around, so if you can take advantage of a spell of settled weather you could have a good trip.

By mid-March the weather is usually becoming more settled and the days are stretching out. Much of the snow pack has become well consolidated, and the crevasse bridges are becoming more visible and stable. Guardians go back up to their huts and the ski mountaineering season starts. Conditions generally stay good through to mid-May with the snow pack consolidating all the time, resulting in a change from powder to spring snow.

The weather isn't always perfect on the Haute Route

After mid-May the skiing high up on the glaciers may be excellent, but the shortage of snow in the lower valleys means long walks with the skis on the back. So the guardians close up shop for a short break before the summer season.

Some huts will re-open in the third or fourth week of June, but many are a little later. To walk the route when there is still a lot of snow is hard, so it is usually best to wait until mid-July when the snow in the lower valleys will have melted. High up on the glaciers the walking will be good provided the snow freezes overnight; there will be little avalanche risk, and the crevasses will progressively open up. As September approaches (and earlier in a poor snowfall year) some of the steeper slopes may be short of snow, resulting in steep scree or unstable rocks, perhaps with a bit of ice. Typical in this respect are: the north side of the Col du Chardonnet and the Plateau du Couloir.

Most of the huts close in the third week of September, and few parties will walk the route after that, because the days are closing in and it means carrying food for the winter rooms.

Direction

Considering all the following factors most parties choose to do the route from West to East, rather than from East to West.

1. Ski descents. When going West-East the following are the best ski descents: Val'Darpette, M Durand glacier, Col de l'Evêque and Col du Chardonnet. The ones West-East are longer and generally are done in better snow conditions.

2. Any short, steep sections are better ascended on foot rather than taken in descent, because it is not only easier and quicker to climb up them, but also, if descended on rope, valuable vertical height is lost which could have been enjoyed on skis. West-East the following are climbed on foot: Fenêtre du Saleina, Plateau du Couloir, Col du Mont Brulé and the Adler Pass – a total of roughly 950m East-West only the following are climbed on foot: Fenêtre du Chamois and the Col du Chardonnet – a total of roughly 250m

3. The lift systems can be used to gain height easily and effortlessly. West-East these are: the Grand Montets cable-car, the Gornergrat railway and the Stockhorn cablecar, giving a total height gain of 3,800m East-West you can use the Felskinn cablecar and the Schwarzee cablecar, giving a total of 2,170 km. So West-East has a net gain of 1,630m

4. Perhaps the crucial factor is the Plateau du Couloir. When taken from West-East it is climbed on foot early in the morning from a hut conveniently placed directly below it. East-West the Plateau du Couloir will not be reached from the Chanrion Hut until midday or early afternoon, which may be a bad time to be descending such a steep south-facing slope.

Avalanches

The main types of avalanche are: dry powder, windslab, wet snow and icefall from seracs or hanging glaciers. The ski mountaineer is at risk from all four; in summer the risk from snow avalanches reduces but that from icefall remains high in places.

By developing the skills (through reading, going on courses, being with a Guide) a mountaineer can assess the level of danger on certain slopes. It may be that the nearest you can get is in terms of 'fairly safe', 'fairly dangerous' etc, and you must then consider the level of risk you are prepared to accept By questioning each slope as he gets to it, a mountaineer is able to build up this expertise.

In assessing the avalanche risk there is a tendency to concentrate solely on what is under the feet without considering the slopes above, and so it is an essential part of route planning to consider the danger of being avalanched from above.

This applies particularly to icefall avalanches which are notoriously unpredictable as the main factor in their release is gravity. Since gravity is constantly present, icefall avalanches can come down at any time of day or night.

1. On the Haute Route two disturbing sights regularly occur, probably through lack of knowledge rather than anything else:

2. people pass unnecessarily close under dangerous areas (eg below seracs or hanging glaciers), and indeed often stop there;

groups, and this applies particularly to ski mountaineers, seldom spread out when negotiating dangerous slopes. It obviously spoils the rhythm to stop and spread a group out, but by doing so only one person need be exposed at any one time to danger.

An ice avalanche falling from the Aiguille Verte across the Rognons Glacier

It goes without saying that all parties doing the Haute Route on skis should be equipped with avalanche transceivers and shovels – and should be trained in their use. It is too late to start reading the instructions when your companions are buried.

Crevasses

The state of an individual glacier can change from year to year and within each year from week to week. Such changes can be dramatic, and a mountaineer must continually assess and re-assess the situation.

A crevasse marked on the Argentière Glacier

The fact that there are tracks down a crevassed glacier means one thing – that someone went down it. Whether they arrived safely home that evening or are in a crevasse is anyone's guess. So while tracks might be useful as an aid to route finding (providing they are going the right way) they give no indication at all as to the safety or otherwise of the crevasses.

This point applies particularly to those doing the route in summer, when the glaciers will either be dry or wet.

A DRY GLACIER is one which has lost its top covering of snow, so the surface on which you walk is ice, usually a greyish colour. The crevasses are clearly defined and easy to see, and it is normal to negotiate these glaciers either with or without crampons, and unroped.

A WET GLACIER on the other hand still has a top covering of snow. Crevasses may be clearly visible, but that is not the point – it is the crevasses which you cannot see, the ones which are hidden by the snow, which are dangerous. It may be that someone put a track in a few days before, passing safely over (unseen) frozen bridges. Since then hot summer weather may have weakened a bridge, and the next person who treads on it goes through. What happens next depends on whether the party is roped and on whether the rope management is good.

It is astonishing how many people walk on wet glaciers in summer without being roped-up, and in doing so they show a callous disregard for human life which is beyond understanding. It costs nothing in time to rope-up and having done so the party should then be safe.

For the ski mountaineer it is slightly different. For a start, all the glaciers will be covered with snow, i.e. wet. But it is likely to be a lot colder in April than it is in August, which means that the bridges are likely to be frozen and therefore a lot safer. Another factor is the skis themselves – one's weight is spread over the full area of the skis, so making it less likely to break through than if one was on foot. And finally there is the fact that when skiing downhill much of one's weight is transferred into kinetic energy forward, with very little weight going onto the crevasse bridge.

On the other hand the ski mountaineer has to cope with two extra difficulties. (1) Some crevasses may be very poorly defined. What appears to be a narrow crevasse may in fact be a wide one with very thin and unstable edges of unconsolidated snow almost meeting each other, so giving the false impression of a narrow crevasse. (2) To tie three or four people together and expect them to ski down a slope, unless they are good skiers and have practised roped skiing before, is likely to be a farce with more problems created than resolved.

So in the ski mountaineering season a compromise is usually looked for, for example:

Uphill
Possible to go unroped if: (a) there is a good track, (b) the glacier is not badly crevassed, (c) the visibility is good, and (d) the temperature is below freezing. If just one of those factors is not present, then rope-up; and if any doubt at all, rope-up.

Downhill
Normally to ski unroped with the leader choosing a line which avoids the crevasses and choosing safe places to stop. The time will come when the leader feels unhappy about this, (e.g. the crevasses have got worse or the light has gone flat, making identification of them difficult). The leader then ropes-up to the next best skier in the party, with at least 25m of rope between them, and maybe 30m. If the leader doubts the ability of the second to hold a fall, another person should join the rope. The rest of the party ski exactly in the tracks of the leader. If things get worse still (e.g. the temperature is high resulting in dangerous bridges), the whole party should rope-up.

ROPING-UP: Wear either a full body harness or use coils of rope to convert a seat harness into a full harness. The minimum distance between people should

be 10m in summer (with an absolute minimum of 8m) and 20-25m for
ski mountaineers. The rope should be kept tight and coils never carried in
the hand.

Stonefall

Hot weather in summer can cause considerable stonefall danger. Any steep snow
slope is prone to this danger and an assessment of each must be individually made,
preferably after getting local advice – e.g. from a hut guardian. It may be that the
slope is simply out of condition and should be avoided altogether, and this applies
from time to time to the North side of the Col du Chardonnet, the Plateau du
Couloir and the snow couloir descent of the Stockji.

Orientation

The directions left (L) and right (R) are used to describe a change in direction by
the mountaineer and are usually backed up with an abbreviated compass
orientation – e.g. 'making a rising traverse L (NW) then head back R (N)'. The
traditional way of describing the banks of glaciers by their direction of flow is not
used, but instead the sense of direction of the mountaineer is used. For example:
'move across L and go up the R side of the glacier' would have been the
traditional method, but in this book it is described as 'move across L and go up
the L side of the glacier'.

Gradings

The traditional Alpine system is used: F facile/easy, PD peu difficile/moderately
difficult) AD (assez difficile/fairly difficult and D difficile/difficult. And within
each grade there are + and – subdivisions. This grade takes in the overall
difficulty, which may vary considerably depending on the conditions. It is
therefore an approximate grade.

For the occasional rock ridges the UIAA numerical system is used. Grade 1 and 2
equate to British Moderate, Grade 3 to Difficult, Grade 4 to Very Difficult/Severe.

The 'S' system is used for snow slopes: S1 is for straightforward tracks; S2 for
gentle slopes; S3 for open slopes up to 35 degrees; S4 for slopes 35-40
degrees, or up to 45 degrees if the exposure is only mild; S5 for 40-50 degrees
where the exposure is serious, or 45-55 degrees in couloirs where there is
little exposure.

Timings

The times are for a reasonably fit and competent party in average/good conditions. The overall 'TOTAL' times allow for rests. The main factors which should be taken into account are: poor weather, heavy snow, difficult crevasses, unfitness, and poor skiing ability. If these combine to give times much in excess of the suggested times, consideration should be given to changing the plans.

For interest, in 1990 Stephane Schaffter (a Geneva Guide) went from the summit of Monte Rosa in 36 hours. He reached the Valsory Hut in 8 hours and had his only rest here (a meal, a shower and 20 mins sleep). From the Valsorey stream to the Valsorey Hut took him 25 mins, and from the hut to the Plateau du Couloir 52 mins.

Maps

The following is a comprehensive list of the maps covering the Haute Route. Those marked * are suggested for the Classic Route. Maps marked (S) are available with ski routes.

Carte Nationale de la Suisse/Landeskarte der Schweiz

1:50 000
282(S) Martigny *
283 (S) Arolla *
284(S) Mischabel *
292 Courmayeur *
293 Valpelline *
294 Gressoney

1:25 000
1326 Rosablanche
1329 Saas
1345 Orsières*
1346 Chanrion*
1347 Matterhorn*
1348 Zermatt
1365 Grand St Bernard
1366 Mont Velan*

French IGN 1:25 000 Chamonix (S) *

There is a special 1:25 000 covering Verbier and the Val de Bagnes. Be careful when using this map as North is offset and is not at the top of the map.

Route Diagrams

On the route diagrams the ski route is shown as a solid blue line and the walking route is as a dotted blue line. Where the two routes are similar, only a solid blue line is shown and cross reference must be made between the Skiing and Walking text in order to get the full description.

Navigation is a crucial skill on the Haute Route – studying the map in the hut.

Clothing/Equipment

By using the huts and relying on sound judgement of weather conditions it is possible to go over the Haute Route with a light rucksack. A light pack means speed, and that means safety – as well as enjoyment. In the ski mountaineering season it is possible to have a pack of only 8 kilos, and in the summer it can be lighter still. Those carrying ropes will have heavier packs, but nobody need exceed 12-14 kilos. The following is suggested as a check list.

SUMMER: normal mountaineering clothing, cagoule and overtrousers (lightweight), longjohns (for sleeping in), spare socks and underwear, gloves and spare, warm hat and sun hat, sun glasses with side protection, suncream (minimum Factor 20), lip cream, water bottle, headtorch, harness, 2 prusik loops, 1 lightweight screwgate karabiner, 1 lightweight snaplink, ice axe, crampons, camera, toothbrush and paste, 40-45 litre rucksack.

SKI MOUNTAINEERING: all of the above, except that ski salopettes are useful (maybe unnecessary to carry over-trousers); also good gloves, balaclava, ski goggles, skis with ski mountaineering bindings, ski mountaineering boots, skins, harscheisen, sticks, avalanche transceiver, 40-45 litre rucsack with ski attachments.

GROUP EQUIPMENT: ropes (9mm diameter is sufficient for glacier travel. A 50m length of 9mm is fairly heavy, so consider 2 lengths of 25m instead. Allow 10m spacings between people in summer and 20-25m when ski mountaineering). Crevasse rescue equipment of at least two lightweight pulleys and one mechanical ascender, 2 ice screws, First Aid, repair kit, altimeter, 2 compasses, GPS, set of maps. In the ski mountaineering season, also: bivouac tent and shovels (ideally 1 per person).

Huts

Huts are normally owned by the Alpine Club of the country (Swiss, French or Italian). Members of these clubs receive a discount on the overnight charge and this concession is extended to members of the British Mountaineering Council

Drying out equipment and enjoying the afternoon sun at the Trient Hut

on production of a Reciprocal Rights Card. During the ski mountaineering and summer seasons the huts are manned by a guardian, and each individual guardian runs his/her hut in their own way. As a general rule the following points should be observed.

1. Make a booking by telephone, preferably a week in advance. Most guardians speak English, but the local Tourist Office or Guides Bureau will always help you.

2. Leave skis outside the hut; leave crampons and ice axes in the entrance (NEVER take them into the living room or dormitories).

3. Leave your boots to dry outside the hut and later put them in the entrance. Use the hut slippers.

4. As soon as you arrive check in with the guardian. Present your Reciprocal Rights Cards (if you have them) and clarify what meals you require.

5. Beds are allocated by the guardian, frequently later on when the guardian knows who is staying and what routes are being done the next day. If someone is tired and needs to sleep, ask the guardian and usually there is no problem in getting an early bed allocation.

6. The guardian will supply all main meals, and drinks and snacks throughout the day. But they also need to eat and have time off, so please respect that and if necessary come back later. In French huts there is a room in which you can cook your own food if you wish. In Swiss huts this is not allowed, so if you have your own food either cook it outside or give it to the guardian to cook. NEVER cook in the living room. Those bringing their own food must bear in mind that the guardian makes his living from the supply of food and drinks, so you can hardly expect to be his most favourite customer.

7. Payment is usually by cash, local Bank cheque or Eurocheque.

8. The dormitories are for sleeping, an obvious point which is frequently overlooked. People may be resting or sleeping at any time of the day, so do please respect that. Rucsacks should be sorted downstairs – rustling poly bags are particularly disturbing – and in some huts rucsacks are not allowed in the dormitories. In the morning the blankets should be neatly folded.

9. However disagreeable the prospect, always use the WC and do not go round the corner. That snow may be used for making your tea, or it may be a favourite place for sunbathing.

Mountain Rescue

Mountain rescue and hospitalisation is expensive in the Alps so insurance is essential. Also carry Form E111 from the Department of Health and Social Security – this entitles you to free emergency care in hospitals of EEC countries.

If help is needed the usual procedure is to get to the nearest hut, which invariably will be equipped with a radio telephone. If the guardian is not there, follow the instructions next to the telephone. Nowadays many guides carry radio transmitters, especially in the ski mountaineering season, in which case direct contact can be made from the site of the accident to the rescue authorities.

To attract attention use the alpine distress signal: 6 consecutive signals (eg whistle blasts) repeated at one minute intervals. Or raise both arms so making a 'Y' shape – YES for help. If a helicopter flies over you and looks as though it intends to rescue you, but you do not need help, the signal is one arm raised and the other extended down by the side of the body.

Subject to the weather, a helicopter is invariably used; and while waiting for it certain preparations must be made. Most important of all is to secure all loose bits and pieces (eg poly bags, clothing etc) as these can be sucked into the intake of the helicopter's engine. If there is an injured person, keep him covered with well secured protection that will not blow around when the helicopter comes in. Get the rest of the party together. Preferably a little way from the casualty, sitting on their rucsacks with everything well secured. Everyone should be briefed to stay still unless instructed otherwise by the crew. By all means take photographs, but do not move position as it is very distracting for the pilot and he has enough to concentrate on without wondering if you are about to decapitate yourself on the rotors in the interests of photography.

One person should stand close to the casualty, back to the wind, arms raised in the 'Y' for YES position. If there is a good landing site in front, so much the better; but this is of secondary importance as the pilot will decide where best to land.

History

Who knows what ancient human remains lay in the ice of the glaciers. In 1991 the Similaun Glacier in Austria revealed what appears to be the well preserved body of a 4,000 year old hunter from the Bronze Age, so maybe there are further discoveries waiting to surface from the ice of the Haute Route glaciers.

It is possible that the Romans crossed the Theodul Pass as Roman coinage has been found there, and the same pass my have been crossed by the inhabitants of Gressoney as early as the 13th century. The Col d'Herens was crossed every year up until 1666 by wretched pilgrims having to cross from Zermatt to Sion, but why they had to go via this high col is a mystery. And on the Tiefmattenjoch between the Dent d'Herens and the Tête de Valpelline 17th century armour has been found. Smugglers used many of the cols, bandits sought hiding in the high mountains, hunters and crystal seekers crossed high glaciers in search of bigger finds.

But it seems as though the honour of crossing from Chamonix to Zermatt for the first time lies not with pilgrims, smugglers, hunters or bandits but with the honourable gentlemen of the Alpine club who in the summer of 1861 crossed via the Col d'Argentière, La Fouly, Orsières, Bourg St Pierre, Col du Sonadon, Col d'Oren, Praraye, Col de Valpelline, Zermatt (ref Vol 1 of 2nd series of 'Peaks, Passes and Glaciers' 1862 by F W Jacomb). For the next twenty years or so this summer traverse of the Alps remained a popular enterprise for members of the Alpine Club; and they must have been hardy people, these English gentlemen, because in those days there were no Alpine huts and their overnight accommodation would have been, at the best, high pasture huts shared with the resident animals. They viewed the next development, skiing, with some disdain. One 'old guard' of the Club was heard to remark: "When God made the hills He intended them to be climbed and not to be used as glorified toboggan runs".

It was Dr Payot who introduced skis to Chamonix in 1897, the year before the first ski descent of Monte Rosa by Oscar Schuster and H Moser. And it was again Dr Payot who on 16th January 1903 made the first crossing from Chamonix to Zermatt on skis. His companions were, like himself, all from Argentière and

Chamonix. They were Alfred Simond, the famous guide, Joseph Ravenl (known as 'Ravenl le Rouge' because of his red beard), and Joseph Couttet. With them went Jean and Camille Ravanel, carrying between them 19kg of camera equipment. On the first day they went from Argentière over the Col du Chardonnet, over the Fenêtre de Saleina, down to Orsières and on to Le Chable. On the second day they went up to the Chanrion Hut. From there they went to the Col de l'Evêque, where they were forced back due to bad weather. At this time there was no Vignettes Hut, so they retreated all the way back down the Val de Bagnes. Going via Martigny and Sion they ended up at Evolene. On the next day they crossed the Col d'Herens and skied down to Zermatt. It was an extraordinary achievement – most parties today would find each of those days prodigiously long, let alone one after the other. And it was January.

In the following month, February of 1903, Dr R Helbing, Dr F Reichert and A Pellaud tried to ski from the Panossière Hut to the Valsorey hut via the Col de Meitin They failed, but went on to cross the Malets de Tsessette Chain, descending to Chanrion. During the Descent Anatole Pellaud fell and lost a ski, and had to return alone to the valley. Helbing and Reichert continued to Arolla via the Cols Mont Rouge, Cheilon and Riedmatten; and then they crossed the Col d'Herens, climbed the Tête de Valpelline, and skied down to Zermatt.

In 1910, on 2nd April, Zermatt to Saas Fee was done for the first time on skis. The party was A Martin, H Rumpelt, and guides Oscar Supersaxo (from the famous Saas Fee guiding family) and Hermann Kronig. They crossed the Adler Pass and climbed the Strahlhorn.

And then in January 1911 (the same year the Amundsen reached the South Pole on skis) came the first crossing on skis of the Plateau du Couloir. The party consisted of Prof F Roget and Marcel Kurz (two of the greatest ski mountaineering pioneers), L Murisier, guiding brothers Jules and Maurice Crettex, and guide Louis Theytax. Their route was: Bourg St Pierre, Valsorey Hut, Plateau du Couloir, Col du Sonadon, Chanrion Hut, Col Collon, Bertol Hut. They then made the first winter ascent of the Dent Blanche before skiing down to Zermatt. This route (without the Dent Blanche) became knows as the Classic Haute Route and considering that Prof Roget was fifty years old at the time, it was an amazing achievement. It was not repeated until 1927.

The Verbier Start was not done until 1926 when Marcel Kurz went via the Mont Fort Hut over the Rosablanche and on to the Dix Hut.

An interesting point about all these early ski traverses, with the exception of Oscar Supersaxo's crossing of the Adler Pass, is that they were all done in

January and February. This is because the early exponents of skiing in the Alps were all mountaineers and they used skis to get around the mountains in winter in order to climb peaks and cross passes. They were exposed to short days, cold temperatures, unconsolidated snow and dangerous crevasses: and they endured these because of two misapprehensions. Firstly they believed that because the crevasses had more snow on and around them that they were safer – not realising that the unconsolidated fresh snow concealed dangerous holes and that bridges which looked safe were much weaker than those in, say, April. One of the first fatal crevasse accidents happened to Louis Theytaz within a week or two of his 1911 first Classic Haute Route – when he was skiing roped on the descent of Pigne d'Arolla when he fell into a crevasse over which several of his companions had safely passed, and the rope broke.

Secondly, they misunderstood the föhn wind. Because it was warm when it hit the southern slopes and because it was warm when it came down on the other side, they understandably assumed it had been warm going over the top and that it had therefore consolidated the snow. They did not understand that in going up the southern slopes it had cooled by expansion, subsequently rewarming on its descent by compression, and that it had therefore been cool high up and had not consolidated the snow. So all these early trips were done on unconsolidated snow – powder and windslab.

Other notable dates (in brackets are first ski ascents).

1785 Mont Blanc (1904 H Mylius, A Tannler, K Maurer, H Zurfluh)
1813 Breithorn (1899 R Helbling, E Wagner, H Biehly)
1854 Strahlhorn (1901
1855 Monte Rose (Dufourspitze 1898 0 Schuster, H Moser) (Signalkuppe 1918 Mario Ambrosio)
1856 Allalinhorn
1858 Dom (1917 Sir A Lunn, Joseph Knubel)
1859 Rimfischhor
1860 Alphube
1862 Dent Blanche. Crossing of Col des Planards
1865 Matterhorn.

Valley Bases

Argentière *1250m*

The most important base for the Haute Route and starting point for both the Classic Ski and Walking Routes. Both in summer and spring there is training terrain which is good and easily accessible (piste skiing, off-piste skiing, crevassed glaciers, walking). The Grands Montets Cablecar (3500m) can be used to gain quick access on training days, for acclimatisation and for starting the Classic Route.

Good skiing and mountaineering shops, two supermarkets, pharmacy, doctor, dentist, launderette. A variety of places to eat out (eg Le Dahu, Chez Luigi's, the Office Bar). The Office Bar also has facilities for leaving messages, a mailing address, sending and receiving faxes.

Occasional banking service shortly to be improved and many shops will change money.

Tourist Office (weather forecast posted in window) and Guides' Bureau.

Access

a. by air or train to Geneva, then
    1. by bus to Chamonix via SATAL (infrequent service taking up to 3 hrs, currently departing Geneva Airport 1600 hrs) or 2. in the ski season by ski coach, or 3. by train via Annemase and Chamonix (several changes), or 4. by train from the airport direct to Martigny, change for Chatelard, Vallorcine and Argentière (more expensive by quicker), or 5. a pre-booked taxi may be cheapest for a group, and certainly quickest.

b. by road via Geneva or Martigny. If the Col des Montets is closed due to snow, cars are allowed through the train tunnel at times avoiding the trains.

c. by coach from London (cheapest but least comfortable).

d. train service Argentière-Chamonix; regular and efficient bus service by Chamonix Bus between Chamonix, Argentière and Le Tour.

Chamonix *1050m*

Much bigger than Argentière with consequently better facilities like banks and more shops. But otherwise there is no advantage in staying there.

Excellent Maison de la Montagne next to the Church – Information Office, Guides Bureau and Metéo (Weather Forecasting Office which not only posts regularly updated forecasts outside, but also welcomes personal callers in need of more detailed information).

Access
see Argentière.

Le Tour *1450m*

The starting point for the Classic Walking Route, this small village thrives in summer with walkers and in winter with skiers. It is very limited in terms of places to stay, shops and bars.

Access
see Argentière.

Champex *1460m*

This is a delightful village with the rather unique restaurant/pension owned by the Swiss Alpine Club. The Classic Ski and Walking Routes come down here after their first sections. A bus service goes via Orsières to start the second sections at either Bourg St Pierre, Fionnay/Mauvoisin or Verbier. Bus times can be obtained from the SAC restaurant/pension; but for a group of, say, 5-6 people it may be that a taxi is no more expensive and considerably more convenient.

Access
by air, train or road to Geneva and Martigny, then by bus to Orsières, change buses for Champex.

Bourg St Pierre 1630m

Most people hurtle past Bourg St Pierre on the Great St Bernard highway, fighting juggernauts loaded with Italian cars bound for the European markets (and German ones bound for the Italian), and at the most stopping for petrol at one of the stations overlooking the village. On Tuesday 20th May 1800 another visitor looked down on this little village. He was also bound for Italy, but the 36,000 men behind him were not the same friendly tourists who go this way today. Napoleon was on his way to the Battle of Marengo and the conquest of Northern Italy and he bivouacked his army at the village. A vast quantity of food was consumed – but no payment made. At Aosta he wrote a form of indemnity, promising to pay the village. But time went by, and no payment was made. The matter was never forgotten and eventually in 1984 the Community Council of Bourg St Pierre presented the French Government with the original bill, together with compound interest. The French Ambassador to Switzerland came to the village, made a speech and presented a handsome bronze plaque of Napoleon. No money was paid, but the debt is now deemed settled.

There are several places to stay ranging from simple self-catering dormitory accommodation to comfortable pensions with beds and good food. One small food/general store which closes on Thursdays for half-day, but the petrol stations on the main road are open and they sell sweets, chocolate and shampoo, which may be the three things you need.

In summer one can choose between staying at Bourg St Pierre or staying at Champex and coming through to Bourg St Pierre early the next morning on the way up to the Valsorey Hut. But in spring it is essential to stay at Bourg St Pierre and to make an early start the next morning, because of the avalanche dangers associated with the climb to the Valsorey Hut.

Access
by road; bus service from Orsières.

La Fouly *1600m*

A staging point on the variations which come down the Orny or from the Grande Lui. It has a well equipped food/general store, a skiing/mountaineering shop, pensions offering beds and dortoirs, and a local guide.

Access
by road; bus service from Orsières.

Fionnay/Mauvoisin.

Fionnay is the last village up the Val de Bagnes, giving access to the Chanrion Hut in summer. It has shops, hotels and pensions. Further up at the road end and perched dramatically below the dam is the small and simple hotel of Mauvoisin.

Access
by road; bus service from Orsières.

Verbier *1500m*

A major ski resort with all facilities, many of which are closed out of season. Starting point of the Verbier Variation.

by road (bus service) from Orsières and Martigny.

Arolla *2000m*

A small and unspoilt village which is busy in all three seasons: skiing, ski mountaineering and summer alpinism/walking. Frequently descended to by those escaping in the face of bad weather from the Dix, Vignettes, Bertol or Bouquetins huts; but also well worthwhile visiting in its own right for a welcome shower, meal and comfortable bed – especially in summer when the route can be continued via the Bertol Hut.

A well stocked food/general store, 2 ski/mountaineering shops, Post Office, hotels, pensions and dortoirs.

Access
by road (regular bus service) from Sion in the Rhône valley. Sion connects via train and road to all the other main centres (Argentière, Geneva, Zermatt, Martigny and Verbier).

Zermatt *1600m*

Until the 15th century it had a Romance name 'Praborgne' (PRATO BORNO, meaning the arable field and the spring). These are now well buried under the glass-fronted fashion boutiques and banks of the High Street and it maybe incongruous that the modern name ZERMATT means 'to the meadow' – further out of town, no doubt.

But despite the development and the huge tourist trade Zermatt has kept many of the old buildings and much of the old way of life. Well worth visiting are the Museum, the churchyard and the Whymper Room at the Monte Rosa Hotel (the room in which Whymper planned his ascent of the Matterhorn). The Matterhorn of course dominates the town, and what a beautiful mountain it is.

Mountaineers from all countries, and especially from Britain, have for many years found a haven at the Bahnhof Hotel opposite the station, run by Paula Biner and her neice Kathy.

Most parties stop the Haute Route here, partly for historical reasons, partly for time considerations and partly because the extension on to Saas Fee is slightly artificial.

The Haute Route

Access

by road and train from Visp in the Rhône valley to Täsch carpark. Visp connects with all the other main centres by train or bus.

Saas Fee *1800m*

A busy all-season resort with all facilities, and for those who continue on from Zermatt it is the final goal.

Access

by road (regular bus service) from Visp via Stalden.

Courmayeur/Entrèves.

These two resorts on the Italian side of Mt Blanc can easily be reached from Chamonix via the Mt Blanc road tunnel. They are used if skiing the Haute Route by the suggested East-West route, or they can be a starting point for a West-East traverse via the Great St Bernard monastery. Entrèves is the actual starting point and has limited facilities, but Courmayeur is only just down the road and has all the shops one could ask for.

Access

a. by road tunnel from Chamonix, or
b. by train, road or air to Milan; then by train or road (bus service) via Aosta.

Skiing: The Classic Route

Argentière – Trient Hut – Champex – Bourg St Pierre – Valsorey Hut – Plateau du Couloir– Chanrion Hut – Vignettes Hut – Zermatt

This is the route which was worked on so hard in the early days, crossing the Fenêtre du Chamois and the Plateau du Couloir. It is the route which has made the Haute Route so famous, and as a ski traverse it has no equal in the Alps. The Plateau du Couloir requires settled conditions and all round ski-mountaineering ability.

Day 1 Argentière – Trient Hut

From Argentière take an early cablecar (about 0830) to Lognan and then up to Grands Montets 3280m. There are three choices of route down to the Argentière glacier.

1. The normal and safest route follows the ski piste down to the point where it bends left at about 3100m; continue off-piste down the glacier on a bearing of 50 True to the rock at 3000m. The IGN 1:25 000 map shows the route passing to the left of this rock, but it is better to pass on its right side, descending on a bearing of 72 degrees True to a broad couloir which is bounded on the left by a moraine, Pt 2754. Descend steeply to about 2600m and then traverse out right and so down to the Argentière Glacier at 2580m Cross the glacier, usually on skins, to reach the foot of the SW ridge of the Aiguille d'Argentière at 2600m.

2. Depending on the state of the crevasses it is usually possible to leave the main piste just below the Col des Grands Montets 3233m and to ski down the Rognons Glacier joining the Argentière Glacier at about 2600m There is some danger from ice avalanches falling from the hanging glacier above the Cordier couloir of the Aiguille Verte, and the actual route varies from year to year depending on the crevasses. Cross the glacier as in route 1.

3. Leave the main piste immediately below the Col des Grands Montets 3233m and traverse R (E) below the north face of the Aiguille Verte to pass just above the rock outcrop 2866m. Traverse a further 200m or so and then ski

Classic Route

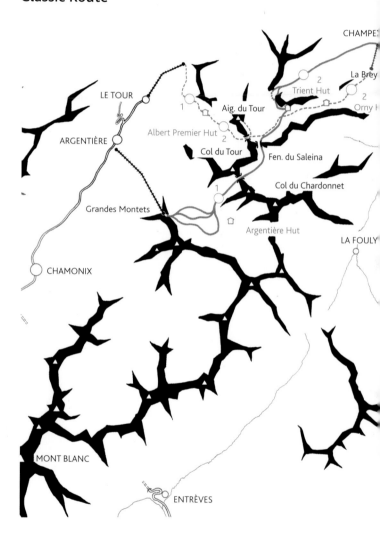

ORSIÈRES

BOURG ST PIERRE

Valsorey Hut

3

Plateau du Couloir

Col du Sonadon

4

Grand St Bernard Monastery

VALPELLINE

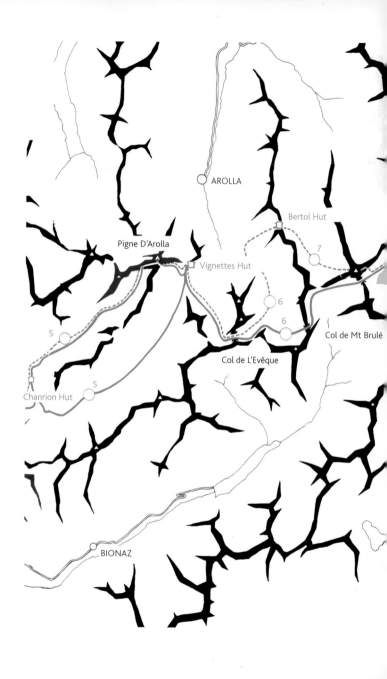

ZERMATT

Schönbiel Hut   8

de Valpelline

ERVINA

VALTOURNANCHE

Classic Route

down to join the Argentière Glacier at c2680m. This route is particularly exposed to the ice avalanche danger from the Aiguille Verte and also to the possibility of falling seracs. In recent years there have been a number of serious accidents and close misses from parties taking this route; but in safe conditions it is a dramatic start to the Haute Route and it brings you down at a higher point on the Argentière Glacier than do routes 1 and 2 enabling you to ski across the glacier without skins to the foot of the SW ridge of the Aiguille d'Argentière.

Skiing down the Rognons Glacier

If there are no tracks and the visibility is poor this point at the foot of the SW ridge of the Aiguille d'Argentière may be difficult to find. It is about 150m below (i.e. NW) of some crevasses on the Argentière Glacier, and there is an iron bar cemented into rock about 20m up the slope. (45 mins-1hr from Grands Montets)

Climb steeply on skins up the lower slopes of the rocky SW ridge of the Aiguille d'Argentière (harscheisen probably useful), moving onto the glacier itself at c2720m Continue steeply up the glacier, keeping to the right of centre (possible avalanche debris from the rocks above), and cross to the centre of the glacier at c2820m passing through some crevasses. The angle eases now and the route continues without difficulty to the Col du Chardonnet 3323m. (2 hrs 30 mins)

The descent of the north side of the Col du Chardonnet is steep and there is a

Gr. Montets

Rock

Route 1

Route 2

Aig. Verte

Route 3

Rognons Glacier

The start of the classic ski route, showing the three routes down to the Argentière Glacier

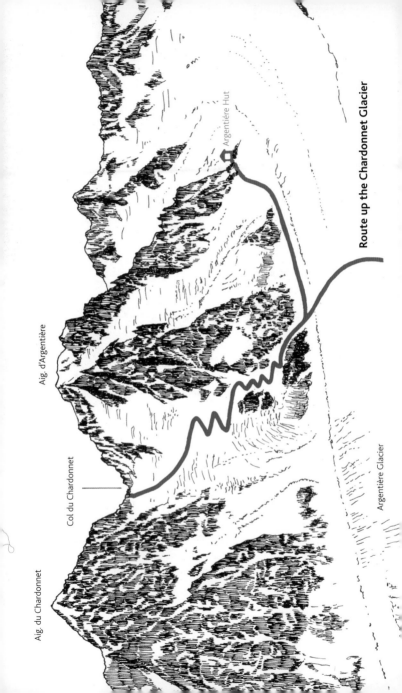

Aig. du Chardonnet

Col du Chardonnet

Aig. d'Argentière

Argentière Hut

Route up the Chardonnet Glacier

Argentière Glacier

bergschrund at the bottom. Most parties side-slip down with the aid of a rope, or climb down. There is a rock belay at the top, or use skis. 90m of rope is needed to cross the bergschrund.

Ski down across the top of the Saleina Glacier to pass just below Pt 3091, at which point the Fenêtre de Saleina 3261m becomes visible. Be careful not to take the first col on the L, the one before Pt 3091 which is the Fenêtre du Tour. The last 30m of the Fenêtre de Saleina are steep and will invariably be done on foot. (1 hr 30 mins)

From the col an easy ski across the upper section of the Plateau du Trient leads to the flat area just West of the Col d'Orny 3098m. Often the best way to ski this is with heel lift but without skins. A short climb on skins leads to the hut. (1hr) TOTAL Grands Montets to Trient Hut 6-7 hours.

To find the Trient Hut in bad weather.
The hut is on rocks directly above a large hole which as been formed initially by recession of the glacier and has then been enlarged by wind erosion. Go up the snow slope to the left of this hole to 3170m, then turn right and traverse briefly to the hut.

If caught by bad weather at the Trient Hut do not attempt to descend by the Combe d'Orny as it is very avalanche prone. All the escape routes from this hut are dangerous after heavy snowfall and the only option available may be to wait or eventually to be helicoptered out.

Alternative Via Argentière Hut.
Many parties split this day by staying overnight at the Argentière Hut. From the Grands Montets use one of the three routes to reach the Argentière Glacier. Climb easily on skins across the glacier, leaving it at 2690m at the foot of a broad spur (marked by two big boulders about 25m above the track), and make a steep, rising traverse up to the hut. (From Grands Montets to Argentière Hut 1 hr-1 hr 30 mins).

To find the Argentière Hut in bad weather.
In bad weather it is easy to overshoot and go too far up the Argentière Glacier, in which case you will find your route to the hut barred by a steep lateral moraine. This moraine, which comes from the Amethystes Glacier, bends through a right-angle as it meets the Argentière Glacier, and the hut is set on the inside of this bend. As you leave the Argentière Glacier at 2690m there are two big boulders about 25m above the track. The rising traverse takes you slightly L to begin with, below these boulders, and then back R below some rocks, with the snow-filled mulde below you on your R. This final section may be icy in which case progress on foot may be safer in order to avoid an involuntary slide into the mulde.

Alternative from Lognan.

If the cable car from Lognan to Grands Montets is closed, the usual route is to go on skins from Lognan, following the marked piste E then SE as far as the viewpoint (Point de Vue) at 2338m. Climb easily up the R (W) bank of the Argentière glacier (some crevasses, but invariably a well worn piste to follow) to join the main route at 2580m (From Lognan to Argentière Hut: 3 hr 30 mins). An easier and quicker alternative is to take the lift to Bochard and then go on skins ENE across the Glacier de Lognan to the col des Rachasses 3037m (the gap with nets where the Pylon piste comes through) from where the normal route is easily reached at the rock at 3000m.

Day 2 Trient Hut – Bourg St Pierre

Judgement of the snow conditions for the descent of the Val d'Arpette will determine the time of departure from the hut. It is seldom worth leaving the hut much before 0800hrs; but on the other hand a late (ie midday or early afternoon) descent will usually result in heavy wet snow and a risk of avalanches from the Aiguilles d'Arpette. The same point applies of going direct from the Argentière Hut (or Grands Montets) to Champex without stopping at the Trient Hut – the snow in the Val d'Arpette may be poor.

Ski down the R (E) side of the Plateau du Trient to reach a flattish area overlooking the steep upper branch of the Trient Glacier. The route traverses out

Skinning over the Plateau du Trient

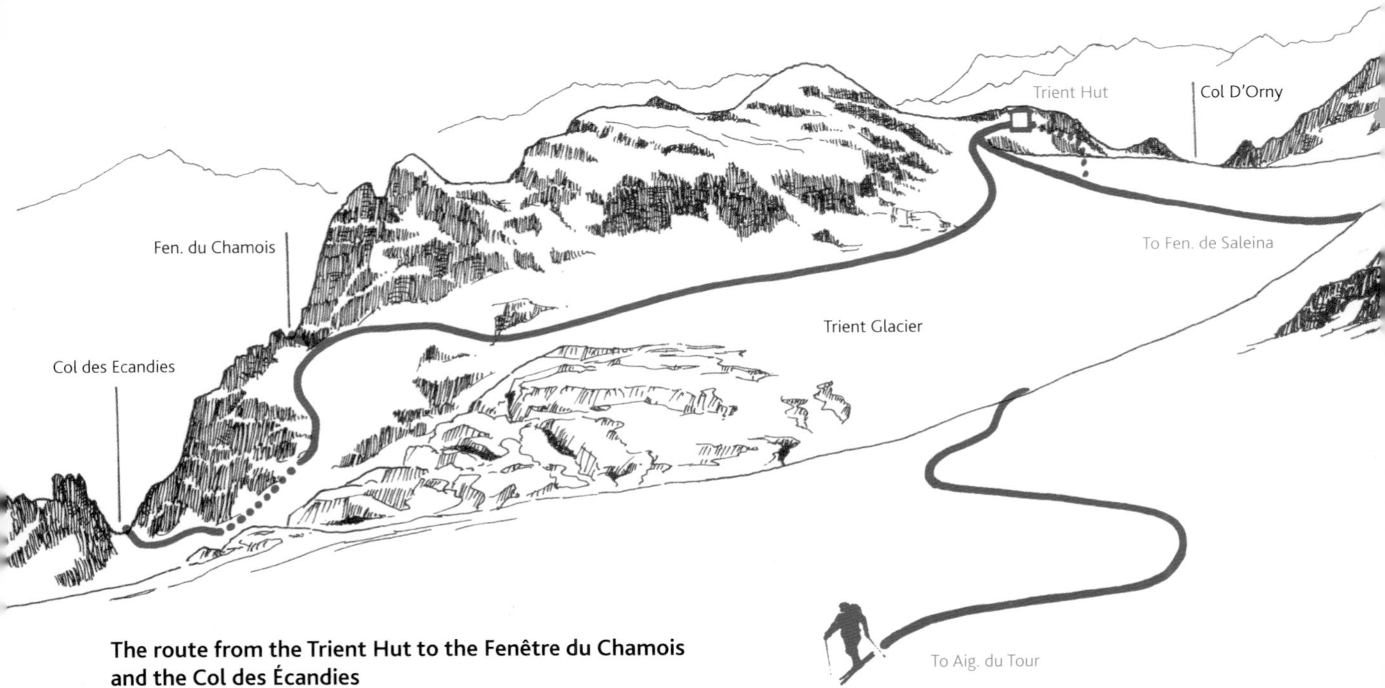

Col D'Orny

To Fen. de Saleina

Trient Hut

To Aig. du Tour

Trient Glacier

Fen. du Chamois

Col des Ecandies

The route from the Trient Hut to the Fenêtre du Chamois
and the Col des Écandies

From Trient Hut

Trient Glacier

To Col des Écandies

Trient Hut to the Col Des Écandies showing the steep descent by the side of the Trient Glacier, and the bergschrund

across this. At the end of the traverse is the small rocky col of the Fenêtre du Chamois 2985m (15mins)

There are now two choices of route:

1. Ski steeply down this upper branch of the Trient Glacier and depending on conditions, either cross the bergschrund (usually well bridged) or move out L onto the glacier to avoid the bergschrund. This movement out L can sometimes be made earlier, when you reach the flattish area. It is less steep but it depends on the crevasses. Traverse R under steep rocks to reach the Col des Ecandies 2796m. (30 mins)

2. When the Haute Route was first done the bergschrund just referred to was impassable, and the route therefore crossed the Fenêtre du Chamois. On its N side this is steep and is usually best descended by abseiling for 100m There is a good rock belay at the top, and a second less obvious one 50m down on the L. This way obviously takes longer than 1. above and requires the right ropes (ideally 2x50m). It is however more interesting and historically was the original way. Also, if route 1. is icy, route 2. may well be a safer option. At the end of the abseil, walk or ski down to the Col des Ecandies. (1-2 hrs depending on the size of the party)

With a vertical drop of 1300m the ski run down to Champex can be one of the best on the Haute Route; but there is a wet snow avalanche risk from the slopes high above on the right, particularly just before and just after passing Pt 1987. In good visibility it is usual to pass over Pt 2195 or just to the right of it, in order to keep height and to ski quickly through the avalanche area. In bad visibility pick up the ridge just to the right (SE and E of Pt 2364; drop down left into the stream bed to pass close under the rocks on the left, and then down to Pt 2280 on the Swiss 1:50 000. Continue past Pt 2100 and on down the valley. This should enable you to maintain a steady rate of descent past the avalanche danger, and it also keeps you as far as possible from the avalanches.

At Arpette there is a road and a Pension. Depending on the snow conditions continue on skis or on foot down through the larch and pine woods, joining a ski piste, and then onto the Champex-Martigny road. Turn R and down the road into Champex village. (1-2 hrs) TOTAL 2hrs-4hrs 30 mins

In Champex on the righthand side there is a Pension/Café called the Relais au Club Alpin and well worth a visit. Transport to Bourg St Pierre will either be by bus (bus stop 50m past the Pension by the Post Office) or by taxi, and helpful advice on this is always obtainable at the Pension.

If you need the bank or any major shopping you should do this in Orsières, since the shops in Bourg St Pierre are limited to one small shop (mini market type selling everyday foods and household goods).

This road section between Champex and Bourg St Pierre is an unfortunate break in an otherwise pure traverse, but it is the way the Route was originally done and is therefore the Classic Haute Route. It is possible to avoid this break by the Grande Lui Variation.

Many do the Classic Route from Argentière to Champex but then by road to Verbier in order to avoid the key section of the Plateau du Couloir – see Verbier Start.

Day 3 Bourg St Pierre – Valsorey Hut

If the mountaineers in the party suffered dented egos on the ski descent of the Val d'Arpette, this is their day. They will love the pain and sweat of a 6 hour ascent, while their skiing colleagues who have not yet acquired the philosophical attitude of the mountaineer will find this day long and unrelenting.

A reasonably early start, say 0600 hrs is recommended. There are several ways leading from the village square out through the closely packed houses and a reconnoitre on the evening before will prevent a pointless pre-drawn circuit of the Bourg St Pierre cowsheds. Pass through a bridge under the main road, and then the path becomes more obvious and is signposted to the Valsorey and Velan Huts. Continue SE up the valley until just below the Chalet d'Amont. On the R there are two bridges over the Valsorey stream – the first goes to a derelict farm chalet, and the second is the summer path to the Velan Hut (signposted). The summer path to the Valsorey Hut breaks off L and climbs up to Pt 2352.5 but do not take this path as it is very dangerous in avalanche conditions. Instead, continue up by the stream until you reach a flat area below the Chalet d'Amont 2198m. (2hrs)

Continue SSE across this flat area following the stream, which may be partly hidden by snow, until you come to the entrance to a gorge which is not obvious until you arrive there. In bad visibility a useful landmark is a 5m boulder with a quartz vein, on the left side of the entrance. Tracks may continue up S to the R of the gorge, but these will be heading to the Velan Hut.

For the Valsorey Hut turn L (E) and climb up through the gorge. If there is not enough snow in the gorge, EITHER go up the next entrance on the R and traverse back to L to the top of the gorge (exposed): OR go further R onto easier ground and then back L round the bottom of the lateral moraine which leads up the Velan Hut (longer but easier). Flatter ground leads to the lateral Velan Hut (longer but easier). Flatter ground leads to the lateral (E) moraine of the Valsorey Glacier. Cross the moraine and continue up over the Grands Plans to Pt 2606m. There are now three choices of route:

1. The lefthand route which bears L and zigzags up the slope to the W of the hut, with a final traverse R to the hut. The whole of this slope is exposed to wet snow avalanches coming down from the Botseresse; and the final traverse towards the hut has avalanched on several occasions after heavy snowfalls. This is the route currently shown on the Swiss maps as the recommended ski route, but this is to be changed in favour of the righthand route.

2. The righthand route ascends the slope to the E of the hut, traversing L (W) when level with the hut.

3. The safest way in avalanche conditions is to gain the rock ridge running down from the hut by going straight up from Pt 2606m, move L and climb on foot up past two cairns to the hut.

(Chalet d'Amont to Valsorey Hut 3 hrs TOTAL 5 hrs-6 hrs 30 mins)

To find the Valsorey Hut in bad weather.
The surest way is to use route 3.

Notes
1. If caught in bad weather at the Valsorey Hut and forced to headback down to the valley, the safest way is to reverse route 3, i.e. descend on foot straight down from the hut to the two cairns, then go R below them and down that slope, regaining the main slope lower down by Pt 2606m. Ski down through the gorge to the lower of the two bridges, i.e. the one which goes to the old farm chalet. Cross this bridge and ski down the L (W) bank of the Valsorey stream where much better snow conditions will be found late in the season than on the R (E) bank. There are one or two sections involving steep sideslips down over bushes and small trees and the Hydro scheme at 1860m may be difficult to pass. Continue down to the chalet at 1740m; then cross to the R (E) bank and follow the road down to the village.

2. By climbing Mt Velan a fit party can enjoy a superb ski mountaineering peak without losing a day on the Haute Route.

Day 4 Valsorey Hut – Chanrion Hut

This is the big day of the Classic Route, the key section finally resolved in 1911 by Marcel Kurz and Prof Roget. Other days are longer, for example Day 6 from the Vignettes Hut to Zermatt, but none have the delicacy of the traverse to the Plateau du Couloir, none have the feeling of commitment which can be felt on the Col du Sonadon, and in bad weather, none have such complex route finding as the descent of the Mt Durand Glacier.

Whether to go from the hut on skis or wearing crampons is often a difficult decision. In fresh snow skis will be best, but if wearing skis there comes a point (often difficult to judge) when to change them for crampons – and the changeover takes time. If the snow is hard it is invariably best to go with crampons right from the hut.

From the hut climb straight up, tending L to the ice boss. Then make a rising traverse R onto the main slope followed by some zig-zags to pass an obvious rock. Continue straight up until it is possible to traverse R onto the Plateau. The point at which the traverse is made varies according to conditions, but is usually well trodden. The last 100m are exposed, it might be icy and there may be a cornice. The slope has avalanched but not as frequently as one might have thought, perhaps because it is too steep (50 degrees on the traverse) to hold snow in quantity. Nevertheless it is definitely a slope to be avoided on a hot afternoon or in windslab conditions. Crampons will almost always be needed, as will ice axes and maybe the rope. There is a rock belay on the plateau, set back on the L but this may well be buried in which case a ski belay will be best. (2-3hrs)

The Plateau du Couloir itself is, as its name suggests, entirely flat – an ice terrace lying under the South Face of the Grand Combin. There is an emergency bivouac shelter on the rocks of Pt 3661. The descent is ESE down a steep slope (100m) onto the upper section of the Sonadon Glacier. This slope is a potential windslab slope. Confident skiers will short swing down it; others may wisely choose to walk down. Traverse L (E then SE) onto the Col du Sonadon Glacier. It may be feasible to reach the col without putting on skins. The col itself lies 50m R of some rocks. (1hr)

From the Col du Sonadon there is an 800m ski descent down the Mt Durand Glacier. There are two choices:

1. The normal route is to ski straight down from the col heading SE and staying on the L of the glacier. Traverse R below an icefall and above a much larger

Making the crucial traverse between the icefalls at 3260-3350m on the Mt Durand Glacier

(but at this stage unseen) one. The point at which this crucial traverse is made varies from year to year depending on the condition of the crevasses, and is usually between 3260-3350m.

2. From the col ski S until just to the S of Pt 3526. Then ski ESE down a steep slope to join the normal route. Normally less crevasses, but steeper skiing.

Head down SE below the Grande Tête de By, then E below the Tête Blanche. At about 3160m the normal route is to maintain a high traverse line on the R below the rocks, all the way down to about 2700m Alternatively go down the middle of the glacier, which can give some very pleasant skiing and may well be the preferred route.

At 2700m head up R off the glacier and negotiate lateral moraines to gain a snow covered terrace which leads to Pt 2735.7, a flat area on a broad shoulder. (1hr)

There are now two choices of route:

1. The normal route is to ski SE past Pt 2655 to Pt 2559; head NNE down steeper slopes; traverse close under rocks to the bottom of the Grande Chermotane basin, ending up in the flat area well to the R (E) of Pt2207, just left of the point where the Otemma stream comes out of the gorge. (30 mins)

Plateau du Couloir

Col du Sonadon

Valsorey Hut and the Plateau du Couloir

Perfect Spring snow on the upper section of the Mt Durand Glacier, with the snow terrace leading to Pt.2735.7 clearly visible lower down

2. Better snow may well be found, however, by staying close to the line of the summer path; then traverse R (E) at about 2400m; down a steepish slope; and finally close under the rocks on the right to finish down in the basin (30 mins).

Climb on skins NNW to the hut (30 mins). TOTAL 6hrs-7 hrs 30 mins

To find the Chanrion Hut in bad weather.
Pass 100m to the R of La Paume and very close to the R of the top chalet . (Le Neuf). The hut is 250m further on, tucked away on a small plateau in the middle of some undulating ground. The Swiss 1:25 000 map is useful in poor visibility as it shows all the chalets of La Paume.

The first hut was built in 1890 from wood and the name Chanrion stems from 'Le Champ Rond', the round field.

Day 5 Chanrion Hut – Vignettes Hut

There are two possible routes.

1. The traditional route goes up the Otemma Glacier, which, despite the magnificent scenery is flat and tedious. It does however enable the route to

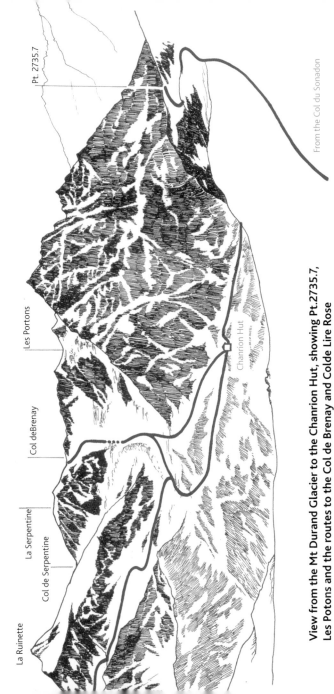

Pt. 2735.7

La Ruinette

Col de Serpentine

La Serpentine

Col deBrenay

Les Portons

Chanrion Hut

View from the Mt Durand Glacier to the Chanrion Hut, showing Pt.2735.7, Les Potons and the routes to the Col de Brenay and Colde Lire Rose

be pushed through to the Vignettes Hut in bad weather. A fit party can bypass the Chanrion Hut and go from the Valsorey Hut to the Vignettes Hut in one day – an observation rather than a recommendation.

From the Chanrion Hut ski SSE back down to the flat area in the Chermontane Basin. Put on skins and climb SE then E up through the Otemma stream gorge. Passing the Hydro scheme dam can be tricky and is normally best tackled on the lefthandside. Head NE up gentle slopes of the glacier, keeping in the middle all the way. From 2860m the glacier curves gradually L (NE). Pass to the L (W) of the Col de Chermontane 3053m and close to the R (E) of Pt 3189.4. The gradient now increases and a rising traverse NE (steep at one point) leads to a snowy gap on a rock ridge – a few metres W of Pt 3162 on the Swiss 1:25 000 map. Traverse N to the Col des Vignettes, then E to the hut. (4hrs 30 mins-5hrs)

2. A far more interesting route is to go via the Brenay Glacier and over the Pigne d'Arolla 3796m.

From the hut either take the lower line of the summer path N to Pt 2522, then NE to PT2624, and on up the centre of the glacier; or (the higher line) work your way up under the lower rocks of the W ridge of the Pt d'Otemma to pass to the R (E) of Pt 2768, then traverse horizontally to pass to the R (E) of Pt 2840.1. Continue the traverse coming onto the glacier at about 2840m to the L (W) of

Early morning on the steep section of the Brenay Glacier between the Chanrion Hut and Pigne D'Arolla.

Pt 2878. Continue NE up the glacier to 2960m – ie between the Brenay Seracs on the R and the rocky S ridge of La Serpentine on the L.

Climb this steeper section of glacier on foot, passing close to the R of the rock outcrop at 3300m. Continue on skins NE up the glacier passing to the R (E) of Pt 3434 and then N to the Col du Brenay 3639m. Make a gentle rising traverse NE to the Pigne d'Arolla Col 3730m (5 hrs 30 mins).

The summit of Pigne d'Arolla 3796m can be reached on skis in a further 15mins and is well worthwhile for the superb views.

The ski run from Pigne d'Arolla to the Vignettes Hut down the Upper Vuibe Glacier is one of the most popular in the Alps, particularly as the Pigne is one of the authorised helicopter landing sites in Switzerland. On a fine day several flights from Sion will result in scores of brightly clad skiers and an atmosphere of carefree relaxation not usually associated with a mountain nearly 4000m high. However the descent of this crevassed glacier in poor weather is a very different affair and should not be underestimated. At 3300m there is a choice of route:

1. The direct route turns L and makes a steep and exposed traverse NNE below seracs to the Col des Vignettes. There is danger of falling ice from these seracs, and since the route seems to be getting steeper and more serious each year it may be that in time it becomes impracticable (1hr). TOTAL 7 hrs 30 mins from the Chanrion Hut to the Vignettes Hut via Pigne d'Arolla

2. An easier but longer option is to ski S from about 3350m down to 3140 m then then L (E) to traverse NE below rocks to reach the snowy gap on the rock ridge a few metres W of Pt 3162 (1:25 000 map). Follow the final section of the Otemma Glacier route to the Vignettes Hut (30 mins longer).

To find the Vignettes Hut in bad weather.
From the snowy gap on the rock ridge W of Pt 3162 continue N on flat ground which falls away to the R then slightly downhill to the Col des Vignettes, which is at the W end of the rock ridge leading to the hut (waterpipe leading to the hut). Pass onto the N side of the rock ridge and then follow it R (E) for a couple of minutes to the hut 3158m.

The first hut was built in 1923 and was known as the Stewart Jenkins Hut after A S Jenkins, an Englishman who stayed at Arolla and climbed regularly with Arolla guides. He funded the first hut, a small locked bivouac hut for use by the Arolla guides. In 1945 the Swiss Alpine Club built a new hut with 45 places and the name was changed. 'Vignettes' is derived from the nearby icefall which in places resembles the very steep terraces of the valley on which grown the small vines of 'vignes'.

Day 6 Vignettes Hut – Zermatt

There are few days in Alpine ski mountaineering to match this one. Firstly it is very varied – a freezing pre-dawn start finishing with a hot walk down through the shaded pine woods of Zermatt. Invariably there is perfect powder snow on the ski descent from the Col de L'Evêque, and inevitably there is perfect porridge later in the day on the descent from the Col de Valpelline. One moment you are climbing steadily on skins enjoying the steady Alpine rhythm perfected over the previous days. The next you are linking fast turns on an open glacier or weaving carefully through crevasses. This day is a long and committing traverse through some of the most outstanding scenery in the Alps – a fitting finale to the Classic Haute Route. It is 30 kilometres (19 miles) long, crosses 3 cols and 7 glaciers, and has 1100m (3608ft) of ascent. It takes about 8 hrs 30 mins, if there is snow down to Furi, otherwise 10 hrs is a normal time and many will take 12 hrs.

The hut should be left early about 0530hrs in order to reach the Col de Valpelline before midday, in time for reasonable snow conditions on the descent to Zermatt.

From the hut carry the skis along the ridge to the Col des Vignettes and a little further until you can put them on and ski down to pass just blow and to the N of the Col de Chermontane (30 mins).

If you have kept your skins warm inside your clothing they will now stick well for the ascent up the Mt Collon glacier. The route varies depending on the crevassese – either (1) head over towards the foot of the ridge running N from the Col de L'Evêque (Pt 3273 on the 1:25 000 map), and then up to the col; or (2) keep to the R (W) close to Pt 3129 and then towards the Col du Petit Mt Collon, before heading L(E) to the Col de L'Evêque 3392m – the usual route (1 hr 30 mins).

Ski down E on gentle crevasse-free slopes. Where the glacier steepens at c 3280m keep R in order to avoid crevasses and pass close to the L (N) of Pt 3263. Easy-angled skiing leads down past La Vierge 3232m. Ski NE down the steeper slope and head E to pass as close as possible below the NE ridge of La Vierge Pt 2938 on the 1:25 000 map. (30 mins)

Pt. Mt. Collon

Col de L'Evêque

Mt. Collon Glacier

L'Evêque

Routes to L'Evêque and the Col de L'Evêque

Climbing the final steep 100m of the Col du Mt Brulé

Climb gently E on skins up the E branch of the Haute Arolla glacier, taking care to correctly identify the Col du Mt Brulé which can be mistaken for the more obvious col which lies to its R (S) and which is the Col de Tsa de Tsan. Head slightly R (S) in orderto approach the final steep slope in a rising traverse from the S. This final 100m slope to the Col du Mt Brulé is steep, is susceptible to avalanche danger and may have to be done on foot. (1 hr 30 mins)

Col de D'Hérens

Stockji

Schönbiel Hut

Zmutt Glacier

Col de Valpelline

Ski route from Col de Valpelline
down Stockji Glacier towards Zermatt

If caught by bad weather between the Col de L'Evêque and Col du Mt Brulé, either descend to the Bouquetins Hut 2980m (small and usually unguarded) or ski all the way down the Haute Arolla glacier to Arolla.

From the Col du Mt Brulé ski down N to pass close below the E ridge of the Pt de la Grande Arête and onto the flat Haut Tsa de Tsan glacier. (15 mins)

The climb up to the Col de Valpelline is deceptive – it takes longer than hoped. An icefall bars a direct line up the Haut Tsa de Tsan Glacier, so head N then NE keeping to the L (N) side of the glacier. Keep climbing ENE up the final steeper slopes to the Col de Valpelline 3568m. (1hr 30 mins)

If you have left the hut by 5.30am you should be at the Col de Valpelline by 1130hrs in time to enjoy reasonable snow for at least part of the descent to Zermatt. From the Col both the Tête Blanche and the Tête de Valpelline can be easily climbed, but will normally be forgone in order to make the best of snow conditions on the descent.

Ski NE down the L (N) side of the Stockji Glacier to c3200m. Much of this descent is heavily crevassed and great care must be taken, particularly with no tracks to follow and in bad visibility. If in doubt keep L rather than R. At c3200m turn R (SE) to reach the top of a steep slope leading down onto the Tiefmatten glacier. The further R (W) you go on this slope the less steep it is, but the greater the danger from falling seracs from above. At 3000m turn L and ski NE down a gentle section until the glacier again steepens at c2940m Keeping well into the L under the rocks on the Stockji, descend to c2660m.

There is now a choice of route:

1. down the L (N) side of the Zmutt glacier. A climbing track to the Schönbiel Hut may be used for fast and committing schusses, but eventually one has to cross the glacier to reach the Stafel Hudro Scheme at Pt 2222 and this last section can be tedious as it contains many dips and humps.

2. cross to the R (S) side of the Zmutt glacier. Taking a high line keep the speed up and ski quickly below the N face of the Matterhorn. Having been in the shade longer, the snow will be harder than in the centre of the glacier, and this route is therefore much faster. However it is exposed to avalanches from above.

Both routes lead to the Stafel Hydro Scheme road at Pt 2222. (1 hr 30 mins)

With good snow cover it is possible to ski on down the road and ski runs using a marked piste which starts at the hotel at Pt 2199, but later in the season it will be a 4.5km walk to Furi. (30 mins -1hr) TOTAL 8-11 hrs

The Furi Cablecar offers a quick and easy descent to Zermatt. Purists, the impoverished and late arrivals will enjoy the path down through the pine woods and first summer flowers.

Skiing: Grande Lui Variation

**Trient Hut – Grande Lui – La Fouly – Great St Bernard Monastery
– Velan/Valsorey Huts**

The road section between Champex and Bourg St Pierre is an unfortunate break on the Classic Route. This variation cuts out that road section and is therefore a much purer line. Nights are spent at La Fouly, the Great St Bernard Monastery and maybe the Velan Hut – so adding one (maybe two) days to the normal route.

On each day steep ground is crossed and the Col de Saleina is steeper and more serious than anything else on the Classic Route. Good weather and minimum avalanche risk are therefore required for this superb route which is highly recommended to competent parties.

Day 1 Trient Hut – Grande Lui – La Fouly

Leave the hut by 0600hrs at the latest and ski down to the Col d'Orny. Climb on skins to the Col Droit (also known as the Col des Plines) between Pts 3294 and 3325 on the N Ridge of the Aiguilles Dorées. The col is deceptively closer to Pt 3294 than Pt 3325 and is obvious from the large cornice invariably there. Descend the cornice at its weakest point, and then ski down the delightful slopes of the Glacier des Plines (steep at first) past the Envers des Dorées bivouac hut 2983m to reach the Saleina Glacier at c2800m. (2hrs)

Pass through crevasses to reach the branch of the glacier leading up to the Col de Saleina 3419m. As you climb up this very scenic glacier two possible cols emerge on the right, followed later by two couloirs behind an obvious rock spire. The Col de Saleina 3419m is the left hand one of them all. The French IGN 1:25 000 map shows the route crossing the Col de la Grande Lui further L still but this is steeper and is not recommended. From the bergschund to the col is a steep slope, about 200m at 48 degrees on which rock belays are scarce. (3hrs)

The Grande Lui 3509m is less than 100m further up, but may be foregone in favour of optimum snow conditions on the descent.

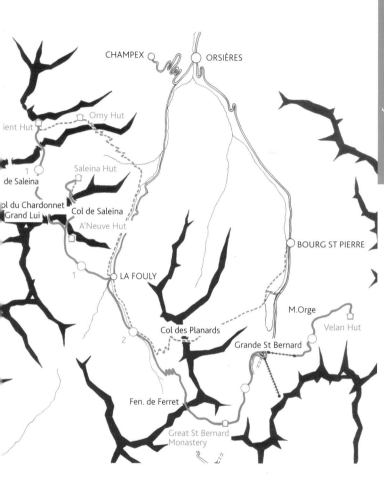

CHAMPEX   ORSIÈRES

Orny Hut

ient Hut

Saleina Hut

1

de Saleina

Col du Chardonnet
Grand Lui

Col de Saleina

A'Neuve Hut

BOURG ST PIERRE

1

LA FOULY

M.Orge

Velan Hut

Col des Planards

Grande St Bernard

2

Fen. de Ferret

Great St Bernard
Monastery

Grande Lui & La Fouly Variations

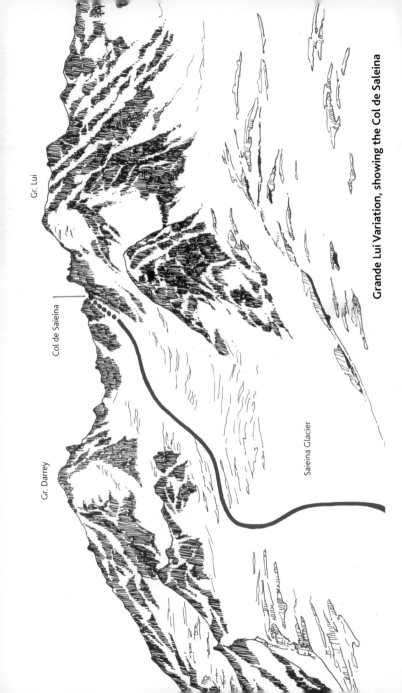

Grande Lui Variation, showing the Col de Saleina

Climbing the steep 200m slope to the Col de Saleina, the crux section of the Grand Lui Variation

The ski descent to La Fouly is 1800 vertical metres, it invariably holds excellent spring snow and there is no equal to it on the rest of the Haute Route. Soon after leaving the Col de Saleina a turn L (E) is made to pass close under the SW ridge of the Petit Darrey. This section is at risk from avalanches from above; but thereafter superb open slopes lead past the unguarded A'Neuve Hut and on down to La Fouly. (1 hr 30 mins) TOTAL 7hrs

At La Fouly there are dortoirs in the hotels, a well equipped mountain shop and supermarket.

The Tour Noir from La Fouly. The 1800m descent from the Grande Lui is down the slopes on the right and appears much foreshortened in this photograph.

Day 2 La Fouly – Fenêtre de Ferret – Great St Bernard Monastery

Depending on snow conditions walk or skin up the road to Ferret and Les Ars Dessous. Follow the line of the summer path to les Ars Dessous and Plan de la Chaux. At 2160m a steepish gully is crossed, probably on foot. Continue up steep ground (probably on foot), right on up to the northernmost lake of the Lacs de Fenêtre – keeping to the line of the summer path all the way (4hrs).

Pass between the Lacs de Fenêtre and climb easily to the Fenêtre de Ferret (1hr). A short ski descent leads to the road which is followed up to the Monastery. (45 mins) TOTAL 6 hr 30 mins

The Monastery was founded in the 10th Century by St Bernard of Menthon on the site of a yet earlier hermitage. Overnight accommodation at the Monastery was traditionally free to passing travellers, but today a charge is made for the unique experience of sleeping in a converted cell and eating with the monks. You may not actually meet a brandy-carrying dog, because the Monastery is so remote in winter that the Great St Bernard dogs are taken down to Martigny where they are guaranteed veterinary care and they return for the summer.

Day 3 Great St Bernard Monastery – Velan/Valsorey Huts

From the monastery ski down the road to Bourg St Bernard (20mins).

Take the Les Darreys Lift to Pt 2273 or if this is not working climb on skins to that point. (45 mins)

Climb E then NE towards the Col de Prox 2779m (2777m on the 1:50 000). This slope becomes very steep from 2460m and the best line is up the gully with the stream. It is possible to traverse L at, or just above the level of the col, but this crosses even steeper and more exposed ground and is not advisable in icy or avalanche conditions. It is best to carry on up to c2810m, then traverse L on flat ground and descend easily to the last steep slope below the col, which will normally be climbed on foot. Possible cornice. (3 hrs 30 mins-4 hrs 30 mins)

From the Col de Prox make a rising traverse R towards a flat ridge above the lake at Pt 2811. Staying on this ridge head NW towards Montorge 2881m, finally using a band of snow to pass between some crags. (1hr)

Depending on conditions the col at Pt 2922 (marked on the Swiss 1:25 000 but not the 1:50 000) may be better and quicker.

Easy slopes and beautiful scenery above the Lacs de Fenêtre on the Grande Lui Variation

From Montorge ski NE down the superb slopes of the Chaux de Jean Max to about 2300m when a traverse R (E) joins the normal route up to the Velan Hut. (45 mins)

Climb by the normal route via the moraine up to the Velan Hut. (45 mins) TOTAL 7 hrs 30 mins

If continuing to the Valsorey Hut, cross the moraine and join the normal route at the Grand Plans. (2 hrs 30 mins) TOTAL 9 hrs 30 mins

Skinning – a great way to travel

Alternative Via Saleina Hut.

From the Col du Chardonnet ski E down the Saleina Glacier, normally passing to the S of Pt 2944. Come off the glacier at c2600m and skin up to the Saleina Hut 2691m. The hut is normally unguarded in Spring, but is open and equipped. From the Saleina Hut there are two ways of reaching the A'Neuve Hut:

1. Head back up the glacier towards Pt 2944 and rejoin the Trient Hut route over the Col de Saleina.

2. From the Saleina Hut climb SSW up the Glacier de l'Evole to the Col des Planereuses 3030m Ski SE down onto the Planereuses Glacier, then S to c2860m climb S then SW to cross the Col de Crête Sêche 3024m – a little

shoulder on the ridge separating the Planereuses and Treutse Bo glaciers. The next col is the Col des Essettes 3160m to the SW. From this col descend a couloir and then make a descending traverse W to pass above rocks, so reaching the glacier just above the A'Neuve Hut to rejoin the Trient Hut route.

Skiing: East to West

Zermatt to Chamonix via Ollomont and the Valleé Blanche

When doing the route East-West it is usually best to avoid the Plateau du Couloir which has to be descended at midday or early afternoon, an unhealthy time to be descending such a steep south-facing slope. The proposed route not only avoids the Plateau du Couloir but finishes with the Vallée Blanche, a fine way of entering Chamonix after a week in such dramatic mountains. West-East tends to have the advantage in terms of ski descents, but this route adequately compensates for this with the descent to Arolla, Les Portons, Mont Gelé and of course the Vallée Blanche.

Day 1 Zermatt – Schönbiel Hut

Take the Schwarzee Lift and then ski down to the Zmutt Glacier via Oberl Stafelalp. Skin up the R (N) side of the glacier and then up the Schönbiel Glacier, finally approaching the hut from the W and not by the summer path which takes the lateral moraine and approaches from the E (2hrs). TOTAL 4 hrs

Day 2 Schönbiel Hut – Arolla

Ski down to the Zmutt Glacier (20 mins) and skin up to the Col de Valpelline following the normal descent route. (3hrs)

A good ski descent (30 mins) followed by a short skin up to the Col du Mt Brulé. (30 mins)

Normally skis are carried down the steep W side of the Col du Mt Brulé. There then follows a superb descent of over 1,000m down to Arolla. There is negligible crevasse problem, and if in doubt keep to the middle of the glacier. (1hr 30 mins) TOTAL 7hrs

Day 3 Arolla to Dix Hut – Vignettes Hut

There are respective advantages to each hut, Pigne d'Arolla 3796 being the objective from both.

Cabane des Dix 2928m. Take the Fontanesses Lift from Arolla. This closes about a week after Easter and then runs three times a day for ski mountaineers, about 0830, 1145 and 1500 – check the times with the Lift Company. From the top of the lift skin up to the Pas de Chèvres 2855m; descend the ladder on the W side and skin easily up to the hut 2929m which is perched on rocks by the (W) lateral moraine of the Cheilon Glacier (2hrs -2 hrs 30 mins).

To find the Dix hut in bad weather:
from the Pas de Chèvres go on a compass bearing of 240 degrees across the glacier (negligible crevasses) to reach the rocks on which the hut is built. Turn L (SW) and climb steeply in a rising traverse R to L up the moraine. At the top turn R (N) and follow the crest of the moraine to the hut.

Mt Blanc de Cheilon 3869m (PD) is an excellent ski mountain, one of the best in the Alps, and is highly recommended as a day tour from the Dix Hut. See Chapter: Mountains.

La Luette 3548m. (PD) is easily accessible from the hut. Its glacier is moderately crevassed and the final ridge is usually done on foot – cornice on the L (W) side. A short but interesting excursion. (Ascent 2hrs, descent 1hr)

Cabane des Vignettes 3194m. Take the Fontanesses Lift from the Arolla. From the stream bed immediately to the S of the lift skin steeply E up and over the lateral moraine of the Tsijiore Nouve Glacier. Cross this easily SE to climb the lateral moraine on the far (E) side. Traverse from R to L up a steep open slope to cross the old lateral moraine at the foot of the Piece Glacier. (Lots of lateral moraines on this route, but that is the last one). Keep R on the W side of the glacier to c2800m, then move gradually over to the L (E) side, and easily to the hut 3194m. (2hrs -2 hrs 30 mins)

To find the Vignettes hut in bad weather:
the final slopes of the glacier steepen to meet a ridge running W-E, and the hut is at the L (E) end of the ridge. On the far (S) side of the ridge is a vertical drop of several hundred metres. If you fall down this you've gone too far, but at least you'll know where you are since the waste from the toilets also goes down here.

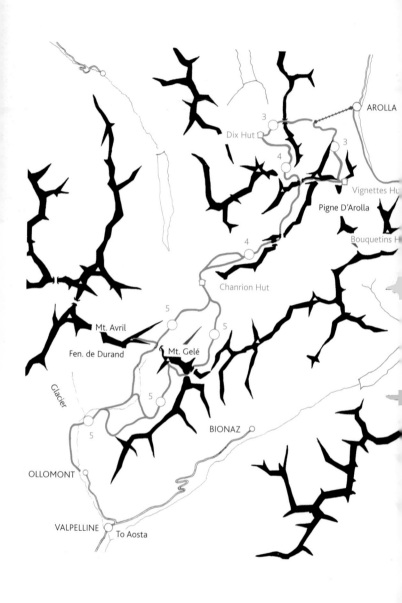

ZERMATT

Furi

Schônbiel Hut

Schwarzee

Col de Valpelline

Col de Mt. Brulé

CERVINIA

VALTOURNANCHE

East – West

Day 4 Dix/Vignettes – Chanrion

From the Dix or Vignettes Hut climb Pigne d'Arolla 3796m.

From the Dix Hut
For a route description see the Chapter: Chanrion-Dix-Vignettes.

From the Vignettes Hut
Either take the direct route, making a steep rising traverse below the seracs to reach the glacier at 3300m, or take the longer but easier route via the snowy gap on the rock ride a few metres W of Pt 3162, then traverse SW below rocks until is possible at 3140m to turn R and climb easily on skins to 3300m. From this point the route continues up the glacier avoiding some crevasses to the Col and onto the summit. (3hrs)

From Pigne d'Arolla ski down to the Col du Brenay 3639m and on S then SW down the Glacier du Brenay to c3300m at which point cross to the L (E) side of the glacier and climb on skins to the Col Nord des Portons 3369m. (1hr)

Descend S then SW below rocks and climb gently W to the col at Pt 3391. A steepish descending L traverse leads to the Col de la Petite Lire 3321m. (30 mins)

Now you have one of the best ski descents in the area – over 400 vertical metres SW down to 2900m From 2900m either:

1. continue SW traversing below the rocks of the Pointe de la Grand Lire and then a descending traverse to pass above Pt 2768, followed by a steep ski down to contour round the W flank of the Pointe d'Otemma, then SW down to the Chanrion Hut (30 mins); or

2. turn R (NW) to ski down over delightful slopes towards the Glacier du Brenay, turning L (W) at 2780m to pass Pt 2624. Follow the line of the summer path SW then S down to the Chanrion Hut (30 mins). TOTAL Pigne d'Arolla to Chanrion, 2hrs.

There are two other routes between the Vignettes and Chanrion Huts:

1. via the Portons without passing over the Pigne d'Arolla. This is recommended as a very worthwhile tour in itself through interesting scenery with a superb ski descent. From the Vignettes Hut reach the Col de Chermontane 3053m and ski down the R (W) side of the Otemma Glacier to 3000m. Climb on skins up a snow ramp below Pt 3065 and above Pt 3082. This ramp develops into a small glacier which leads easily up to the col at Pt 3391. (2hrs)

The Vignettes Hut

2. down the Otemma glacier, a useful alternative in bad weather but tedious in soft snow due to the gentle gradient.

There are also two other routes between the Dix and Chanrion huts:

1. up the de Tsena Réfien Glacier to the Col de la Serpentine 3547m and then down the Serpentine Glacier – a straightforward and enjoyable descent.

2. cross the three cols of Col de Cheilon, Col du Mt Rouge and Col de Lire Rose. The route is described in reverse in the Chanrion-Dix-Vignettes variation.

Day 5 Chanrion – Mt Avril/Mt Gelé – Entrèves

Ski down into the gorge and then climb on skins SW up the Glacier de Fenêtre (which does not have much remaining glacier) to the Fenêtre de Durand 2797m (2 hrs 45 mins). Climb Mt Avril 3346 by its E Ridge (PD+, 1hr 30 mins) and return to the Fenêtre de Durand. (45 mins). It may be possible, instead of going right to the col to make a rising traverse from c2700m up the E flank of Mt Avril, climbing the final steep rocks on foot. From the col ski SW down the stream bed of the Aqua Blanca past A Thoules to the bridge at 2200m. Continue down W on the S side of the stream for a further 500 horizontal metres to c2100m and then turn L to ski SW down the steep line of the summer path to Glacier 1549m. (1hr; TOTAL 7-8 hrs)

Continue down the road to Ollomont 1356m and then take road transport via Aosta to Courmayeur and Entrèves.

A slightly longer and excellent alternative is to climb Mt Gelé by its SE flank (PD). From the Chanrion hut ski down and pass SE through the gorge, to turn R (S) past Pt 2423 and on up the Ayace valley to the Glacier de Crête Sêche. Cross the steep Col de Ayace which is unmarked on the Swiss 1:50 000 but which lies to the R (NW) of Pt3061. Traverse the glacier horizontally WSW to pass below some rocks, then climb R (W) to cross the rock ridge at its easiest point. Climb NNW then NW up the Glacier du Mt Gelé and up to the summit 3518m. (5hrs)

The descent is S down the Glacier du Mt Gelé to 2800m then R (NW) to find a steep open slope lying between two streams to the N of Lac Beuseya. This slope leads down to the Acqua Blanca where it joins the descent from the Fenêtre de Durand at c2240m below A Thoules.

East – West 2.

Alternatively continue from 2800m SW to the Lage dell Incliousa, then NNW down to the bridge at 2200m where the descent from the Fenêtre de Durand is joined.

Day 6 Entrèves – Chamonix via the Vallée Blanche

The Vallée Blanche is a 17 kilometre long run through some of the best scenery in the Alps and with a vertical height drop of 2750m it is one of the biggest runs in the world. The majority of the run is on glaciers and is off-piste – i.e. there is no ski patrol and no markers – but in fine weather the track is very obvious and will be well pisted from the large numbers who have gone before. The best way to do the Vallée Blanche is on a fine day with a knowledgeable companion who can point out the mountains, take a picnic and a bottle of wine; and enjoy the easy but dramatic skiing. A word of warning though, it is a crevassed glacier and the usual precautions should be taken.

The route can be started from either the French or the Italian side, and when doing it as part of the Haute Route East-West the Italian start is used.

The French Start.
Take the cablecar to the top of the Aiguille de Midi 3800m. To get down onto the glacier there is an exposed snow arête (who hasn't heard of it?). Fixed ropes are put on it in the skiing season and crampons are not usually required. In summer the ropes are taken down and crampons are a good idea. After the arête ski S below the S Face of the Midi; back E to pass close to the Gros Rognon; then S towards the foot of the Pyramide du Tacul. Turn L (N) to join the Italian Start.

The Italian Start.
Take the cablecar system from Entrèves to Pointe Helbronner. The route starts with a traverse NW to the Col des Flambeaux 3407m and continues down easy glacier slopes turning progressively N to meet the French Start. An alternative (and recommended) start from Pointe Helbronner is to head NE towards the Aiguille de Géant; at c3300m turn L (N) to pass through some crevasses; then L again (NW) to come in below La Vierge and so join the normal route.

The route continues N down easy glacier slopes towards the foot of the Petit Rognon and the Géant icefall. This icefall is the steepest section of the Vallée Blanche. There are invariably open crevasses here and sometimes the movement of the glacier can throw up steep sections (even requiring the use of a rope). Great care is needed: do not turn over a blind drop as it might conceal an open crevasse on the far side, and watch out for other skiers who might be skiing without the required control and who could knock into you.

Below the Géant icefall is the Requin Hut out on the L. This makes a good stopping place, or ski down to the flat area below the hut (the Salle à Manger) which is as good a picnic spot as you will ever find.

From the Salle à Manger the angle of the glacier eases right off and there are numerous small variations which can be taken. In summer when the Montenvers railway is running the glacier is left here and the railway taken down to Chamonix. In the skiing season continue down the glacier to c680m. Leave the glacier on the L below a steep ice drop and follow a path gently uphill for 10 minutes to a small hut selling drinks etc. An obvious path contours round the hillside and leads right down to Chamonix. If the snow lasts you will ski all the way down, and if it runs out you will have an enjoyable walk – just how enjoyable depends on the comfort of your boots.

Skiing: Chanrion Hut – Dix Hut – Pigne D'Arolla – Vignettes Hut

If time permits (it adds an extra day) a worthwhile diversion is to cross from the Chanrion Hut via the Col de Lire Rose, Col du Mont Rouge and Col de Cheilon to the Dix Hut. Then there is a varied and superb day crossing Pigne d'Arolla to the Vignettes Hut.

Day 1 Chanrion Hut – Dix Hut

From the Chanrion Hut take the lower line past Pts 2522 and 2624; continue up the Brenay glacier to about 2700m; then turn L (N) to climb steeply to the Col de Lire Rose 3115m. (2 hrs 30 mins)

Traverse NNE into the bowl of the Lire Rose Glacier, and then climb N to the Col du Mont Rouge 3325m. The last 80m of this S facing slope can be dangerous with windslab and cornices after N winds. The rock is loose, and there have been a number of serious avalanche incidents here (1 hr-1hr 30 mins).

Traverse NE across the flat upper section of the Gietro glacier to reach to Col de Cheilon. (30 mins)

Ski NE down the easy slopes of the upper Cheilon glacier, passing to the L (W) of Pt 2986 – the Swiss 1:50 000 shows the route incorrectly passing to the R (E) of this point. A short traverse and ascent leads to the Dix Hut 2928m (1hr; TOTAL 6 hrs)

The hut is named after the ten ('dix') bandits who, according to legend, operated from the Val des Dix. From time to time they went into the mountains for hiding and shelter, using the area where the hut is built.

Mt Blanc de Cheilon 3869m can be climbed on the way and is well worthwhile for strong parties although it will more likely be done in a separate day from the Dix Hut. See Chapter: Mountains.

Day 2 Dix Hut – Pigne d'Arolla – Vignettes Hut

Ski down from the Dix Hut onto the Cheilon Glacier which is crossed on skins. Climb the de Tsena Réfien Glacier on the L side, finally passing close to the R (W) of Pt 3423. The way ahead looks improbable: continue SW towards the Col de la Serpentine: at 3500m turn L (E) and contour in to below a steep slope – the bit which looks improbable. Climb this in a steep rising traverse from R to L – possibly on skis, but invariably safer on foot with crampons as it can be icy. Gentle slopes lead SE to the Col de Brenay 3639m, then ENE to the Pigne d'Arolla Col. (4-5 hrs)

The summit of Pigne d'Arolla 3796m can be reached on skis in a further 15 minutes.

For the descent to the Vignettes Hut see the Chapter: Skiing, The Classic Route.

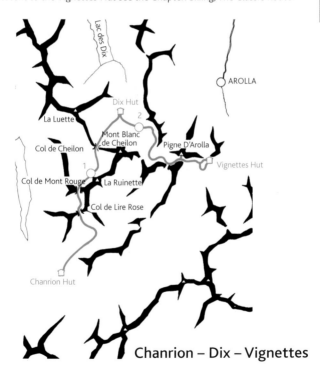

Chanrion – Dix – Vignettes

Skiing: Verbier Start

Many parties start the Classic Route and then at Champex they go by road to Verbier in order to make this connection to the Dix Hut, followed by the route over the Pigne d'Arolla to the Vignettes Hut. It offers a useful alternative if the Plateau du Couloir is in dangerous condition and a chance to push the route on to Zermatt. There can, however, be a considerable avalanche danger when traversing above the Lac des Dix.

Day 1 Verbier – Mont Fort Hut

Use the Verbier Lift system to gain a short ski run down to the Mont Fort Hut 2457m. Many options are available depending on which lifts are running, with Les Attelas offering as direct a route as any.

Day 2 Mont Fort Hut – Prafleuri Hut

Climb on skins SE to the Col de la Chaux 2940m. (1 hr 30 mins) A short ski descent SE is followed by another climb to the Col de Momin 3003m (1 hr 30 mins). Continue ESE onto the upper part of the Grand Desert Glacier to c3160m at which point turn R if doing the Rosablanche or turn L to ski NE down the Glacier de Prafleuri to the Prafleuri Hut, which is normally unguarded in the ski mountaineering season. Take coins for the electric meter. TOTAL 4 hrs 30 mins, plus 1hr for the Rosablanche

Day 3 Prafleuri Hut – Dix Hut

Climb to the Col des Roux 2804m, then ski S down past La Barma and continue traversing above the Lac des Dix to Pt 2386 Pas du Chat. Climb gently E below rocks, then SE to Pt 2581. Follow the stream bed S to the Dix Hut (5 hrs).

It is possible to go from the Mont Fort Hut to the Dix Hut in one day, so avoiding the unguarded Prafleuri Hut. There are two routes, both giving a long day and both exposed to considerable avalanche risk as you traverse above the Lac des Dix late in the day.

Just before the Col de Momin go R (SE) to traverse below rocks up to the col at Pt 3039 (Col de la Rionde on the 1:25 000 map). Continue E then SE to the Col de Severeu 3111m. Ski E then NE down the Glacier des Ecoulaies to La Barma where the normal route is joined.

Traverse the Rosablanche by descending the SW ridge to Pt 3241. Ski down the Glacier de Mourti to La Barma where the normal route is joined.

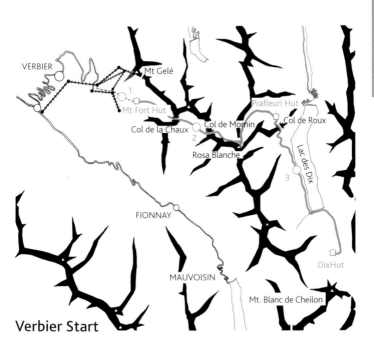

Verbier Start

Skiing: Courmayeur – Great St Bernard Monastery

This is an interesting connection between Courmayeur and the Great St Bernard Monastery and is here described West-East although it can be done in either direction. By using the Mont Blanc tunnel or the Vallée Blanche it can be used as a connection between Chamonix/Argentière and Bourg St Pierre.

Go up the Val Ferret as far as La Vachy 1642m. Climb on skins SE to Malatra and continue to the R (S) side of the stream (the summer path is on the other side), to c2530m when a rising traverse can be made to the L (NE) above the rocks and on to the Col Malatra 2928m.

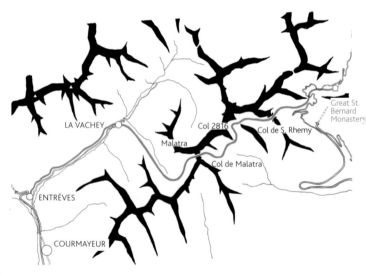

Courmayeur – Great St Bernard Monastery

Ski down the foot of the rocky ridge running SE from M Tapie, following the line of the summer path. Traverse across at c2480m to pass below the rocky ridge running SE from Bella Comba. Climb N and then NW between this ridge and the stream on the R to c2750m and then head NE to the unnamed col at 2186m. Ski E down the comba La Tula to cross the Col S Rhemy 2560m Ski down NE and E to pass the huts at Pra de Farco; and then down to the old road; and so up to the monastery.

Skiing: Zermatt – Saas Fee

Historically the Haute Route finished at Zermatt as all the early traverses ended there. Continuing on to Saas Fee extends the trip by one or two days, depending on whether you stay at the Britannia Hut, and gives some good ski mountaineering with the option of bagging a 4,000m peak, the Strahlhorn. If the time is available a decision has to be made on whether to do Zermatt-Saas Fee or whether to do one of the other options, eg Mont Velan, Chanrion-Dix-Vignettes, the traverse of the Grande Lui, Monte Rosa or Mont Blanc. Zermatt-Saas Fee is made relatively easy by the Stockhorn Lift, and if this is not running (it closes about 2 weeks after Easter and remains closed for the whole of May – see telephone list for contact number), it becomes a 3 day trip.

Three routes are given. Route 1 is the normal route and is invariably used if the Stockhorn Lift is working. Route 2 is not only useful if the Stockhorn lift is closed, but gives an easy 4000m peak (the Breithorn) and a magnificent descent – and also the chance of Monte Rosa. Route 3 via the Täsch Hut offers a quick route in late season.

Route 1 Zermatt – Stockhorn Lift – Adler Pass – Saas Fee.

Day 1 Zermatt– Stockhorn– Adler Pass – Britannia Hut

Take the earliest train to Gornergrat (about 0710 but check at the station), followed by the 2-stage cablecar to the Stockhorn Terminus 3405m. It is usual to carry skis up to the summit of the Stockhorn 3532m. Ski down E, passing to the L (N) of Pt 3462 to the Stockhorn Pass 3398m. Ski down E, passing to the L (N) of Pt 3462, to the Stockhorn Pass 3398m, unnamed on the 1:50 000 map but named on the 1:25 000. (45 mins from the Stockhorn Terminus)

Turn L (N) to ski down the superb upper slopes of the Findeln Glacier where excellent spring snow can frequently be found. Traverse off R to come under the

Zermatt – Saas Fee

rocks below Pt 3421 (crevasses). The steep slope ahead leads on to the Adler Glacier and may have to be done on foot with crampons and ice axe. Climb the Adler Glacier NE on skins, heading near the top towards the rock on the L, in order to take the final slope from L to R, finally coming back L to the actual pass. This top steep-section may be icy, in which case it will be better on crampons keeping in to the rocks on the L. After N or E winds there may be a considerable build-up of windslab. (3hrs)

From the Adler Pass the Strahlhorn 4190m can be climbed by its NW Ridge, depending on conditions either on foot up the ridge or on skis using the snow slopes to the L (N). (1 hr 30 mins) Descent to the Adler Pass by the same route (30 mins).

Ski N then NNE down the easy angled slopes of the Allalin Glacier. At c3460m move towards the middle of the glacier to get the best line through crevasses. Continue NE down gentle slopes past Pt 3258 to close by Pt 3143.3. Cross the Hohlaub Glacier NE and climb the final steep snow slope on skins to the Britannia Hut 3029m. (1hr 30 mins) TOTAL 8hrs from the Stockhorn Terminus and including the Strahlhorn.

Day 2 Britannia Hut – Saas Fee

There is a wide horizontal track from the hut to the Egginer Joch, which may be partly covered in places by debris from small avalanches coming down from the rocks above. If the track looks smooth with no debris it is probably best to go on skis without skins, but with heel lift. If, however, there is debris or the track looks rough, it may be best to have the skins on.

From the Egginer Joch ski NW down the wide gully to join the pistes, and so easily down to Saas Fee. (1hr 30 mins-2hrs)

Many parties make a long day of it and go straight through to Saas Fee without stopping at the Britannia Hut.

Route 2 Zermatt – Klein Matterhorn Lift – Monte Rosa Hut – Monte Rosa – Alder Pass – Britannia Hut – Saas Fee

Day 1 Zermatt – Klein Matterhorn Lift – Breithorn – Monte Rose Hut

Take an early lift up the Klein Matterhorn and ski down to the Breithorn Plateau 3802m. Cross the Plateau E on skins towards the S flank of the Breithorn. All of this flat section looks innocuous enough but beware of crevasses. Head L (N) to make a steep rising traverse up the final slope, coming back R (E) to the summit of the Breithorn 4165m. Depending on conditions, skis may be left at the end of the rising traverse or worm right to the summit. (1 hr 30 mins)

Ski back down to Pt 3802 and then ski down the piste W then N until level with Pt 3201. Turn R (E) off the piste to ski down the Unterer Theodul Glacier. There is a crevassed zone between 3060-3000m which is best taken by going R then back L. The rest of the run is delightful and crevasse free. At c2600m it may be best to head R onto the lateral moraine and ski down that for a while before returning to the glacier and skiing down to Pt 2536. (1hr 30 mins-2hrs)

Put on skins and skin easily up the gentle Gorner Glacier, heading SE onto the lower slopes of the Grenz Glacier and making a final rising traverse through crevasses to the Monte Rosa Hut 2795m. (2hrs) TOTAL from the Klein Matterhorn Lift 6 hrs

An alternative and harder route is the descent of the Schwärze Glacier from the Schwarztor 3734m. The line is basically down the R (E) side passing close to the L (W) of Pts3398 and 2939, but the middle and lower sections of this glacier can be very crevassed and local advice (eg the guides' Office, Zermatt) should be taken on the current condition of the glacier before going on this route. It can give a superb descent and a quick way to the Monte Rosa Hut.

Day 2 Monte Rosa

If conditions are right few people will pass by the opportunity of climbing Monte Rosa, even if it means jeapordising the way on to Saas Fee. For a route description, see the Chapter 'Mountains'.

Day 3 Monte Rosa Hut – Adler Pass – Britannia Hut

Take the Monte Rosa climbing line SE from the hut as far as 2960m, then bear L (NE) to traverse the Monte Rosa Glacier from Pt 3012 to just L (W) of Pt 3081. Ahead is a rock ridge which is climbed, usually on foot, by a N rising traverse, crossing the crest at c3150m. This brings you onto the Gorner Glacier and straightforward skinning NE to the Stockhorn Pass 3398m. (2 hr 30 mins)

Join the Zermatt-Stockhorn Lift route to the Britannia Hut. (7 hrs) TOTAL 9 hr 30 mins including the Strahlhorn

Day 4 Britannia Hut – Saas Fee

See route description above.

Route 3 Zermatt – Täsch Hut – Saas Fee

The Täsch Hut is a dangerous hut to get to in Winter and early Spring due to the avalanche risk, but after mid-season may well be feasible and then offers a quick and direct route through to Saas Fee, as well as giving the opportunity to climb the Alphubel, a 4000m peak and good ski mountain with an interesting descent which is tricky in bad weather due to the numerous crevasses.

Day 1 Zermatt – Täsch Hut

From Täsch take the road through Täschberg and Resti to the Täschalp Hotel 2170m (2hrs). If there is little snow follow the summer approach by continuing on the road, then path, SE past Ottavan and across the Rinderberg to the Täsch Hut 2708m. (1 hr 30 mins) TOTAL 3hrs 30 mins-4hrs

If there is too much snow for the summer route, follow the Mellichbach stream to its junction with the Kummi-Bodmen stream. Climb this steeply and almost certainly on foot to c2600m, then turn L (NNW) and climb more easily to the hut. In bad snow conditions this climb is dangerous and should be avoided.

Day 2 Täsch Hut – Alphubeljoch – Saas Fee

Ascend E past Pt 3052 to the Alphubel Glacier and continue to the Alphubeljoch 3782m. (3hrs)

Ski NE then diagonally N down the glacier to c3400m where the main Langfluh-Alphubel track may be met. Continue basically NE straight down the glacier to Langfluh with suitable detours to avoid the numerous crevasses. One way of avoiding the lower crevasses is to cut R (SE) at 3180m and pass through the snowy crevassed gap between the rock ridge and Pt 3173.7. This leads to easy ground and the piste down to Langfluh. (1 hr 30 mins) TOTAL 4 hrs 30 mins-5 hrs

If climbing the Alphubel, make a rising traverse NW from the Alphubeljoch to 3900m. Continue NW up the steep slope ahead (crevasses), turning L (W) at 4100m to the summit of the Alphubel 4206m. (1 hr 30 mins; 5 hrs from the Täsch Hut). The descent is E down to the foot of the step section at 3900m, then NE down the glacier to 3400m and on down to Langfluh (2hrs) TOTAL Täsch Hut-Alpuhubel-Langfluh 7 hrs 30 mins

From Langfluh ski down the piste to Saas Fee if there is enough snow and if you feel like more skiing, or take the cablecar to Spielboden and bubblecar down to Saas Fee.

Walking: The Classic Route

**Argentière – Albert Premier Hut – Champex – Bourg St Pierre
– Valsorey Hut – Plateau du Couloir– Chanrion Hut – Vignettes Hut
– Bertol Hut – Schönbiel Hut – Zermatt**

Most parties in summer start the Haute Route via the Albert Premier Hut and there are two reasons for this. Firstly, it gives a gentle start to the trip without technical difficulties; and secondly, it avoides the Col du Chardonnet which, in summer without good snow cover, is loose and unpleasant. The route then goes on to cross the Plateau du Couloir, thereby maintaining a purist line.

Day 1 Argentière – Albert Premier Hut

From the village of Le Tour 1453m (regular bus service between Chamonix-Argentière-Le Tour) either take the path ENE direct to the hut which is steep and exposed in places with fixed chains, and can hardly be recommended (4hrs); or go the usual and far more pleasant way which is via the 2-stage Charamillon-Col de Balme Chairlift, then the good path S to Pt 2329, the SE to Pt 2484 and up the moraine to the hut. (1 hr 30 mins from the top lift station to the hut)

King Albert opened the first hut in 1930 to mark the centenary of Belgium independence, hence the name.

Day 2 Albert Premier Hut – Champex

In good weather there will be a track SE up the Le Tour Glacier passing either side of Pt 2883 and continuing to the Col du Tour 3281m. It is however quicker and easier to cross the Col Superior du Tour 3289m (named and spot heighted on the French 1:25 000 map , but spot heighted only as 3288m on the Swiss 1:50 000 map), lying just to the L (W) of the Col du Tour (1hr 30 mins)

The S summit of the Aiguille du Tour 3542m can easily be climbed from here: go N up the Trient Plateau until below the bay between the S and N summits (30 mins). Cross the bergschrund, then easy snow and scrambling lead to the summit (1hr, 3-3 hrs 30 mins from the hut)

Cross the Trient Plateau ENE to the Col d'Orny 3098m (30 mins); then go E down the Glacier d'Orny to the Cabane d'Orny. Continue E to the Lac d'Orny, then E and NE along the path which leads to the top of the Breya Lift 2188m. Take the chairlift down to Champex (this works on the hour, is closed the rest of the time, and is closed for 1hr 30 mins at midday). (2hrs) TOTAL 4 hrs 30 mins, with Aiguille du Tour 6hrs 30 mins-7hrs

Either stay in Champex, a beautiful village, and go on to Bourg St Pierre in the morning; or carry on to Bourg St Pierre where there is also a choice of accommodation. Buses and taxis are available, and the Relais d'Arpette (owned by the Swiss Alpine Club) is a useful source of information.

Day 3 Bourg St Pierre – Valsorey Hut

The path goes SE up the Valsorey valley to the Chalet d'Amont 2198m. From there it makes a rising traverse SE up the slope behind the Chalet d'Amont, passes rocks to Pt 2352.5 and on to the Grands Plans 2501.8. The preferred track is the higher one and is well marked; the lower track is obsolete with old fixed chains. From the Grands Plans the track is well marked up the L side to the Valsorey Hut 3030m. (TOTAL 3hrs 30 mins-5hrs)

If caught by bad weather at the Valsorey Hut it is still possible to get round to the Chanrion Hut in a day by: buses run three times a day from Bourg St Pierre to Aosta; bus Aosta to Ollomot and on to Glacier; taxi Glacier to A Thoules 2378m, 3 hour walk over the Fenêtre du Durand to the Chanrion Hut.

Day 4 Valsorey Hut – Plateau du Couloir– Chanrion Hut

In summer the climb and traverse to the Plateau du Couloir will present no difficulty to a competent party, provided there is snow on it. Later in the season there may be nothing but ice and scree, or just scree; in which case it becomes quite a serious proposition for even competent parties.

From the hut follow the track up, zig-zagging up the main slope to pass an obvious rock, and make an exposed traverse R to the Plateau du Couloir. (2hrs; 3hrs under scree conditions)

Cross the Plateau du Couloir SE to descend a short steep slope down onto the Sonadon Glacier. Traverse L (E then SE) to the Col du Sonadon 3504m. (1hr)

The exact line down the Mont Durand Glacier depends on the condition of the crevasses but generally follows the normal ski route - i.e. go straight down from the col heading SE and staying on the L of the glacier. Traverse R below an icefall and above a much larger (but at this stage unseen) one. The point at which this crucial traverse is made varies from year to year depending on the condition of the crevasses and is usually between 3260-3350m Head down SE to pass below the Grande Tête de Bey and Tête Blanche. Then there is a choice:

1. Come off the glacier at 2700m and go along an obvious terrace to reach Pt 2735.7. Follow the track down through the Grande Chermontane to the bridge (2185m on the 1:25 000).

2. Continue down the R (E) bank of the glacier to the Tsè Bourgo and pick up the path which leads down to the bridge.

Follow the path up to the Chanrion Hut 2462m. (TOTAL 7-9 hrs)

Alternative
If the Mt Durand Glacier is too crevassed, a good option is via the Col du Meitin. From the Valsorey hut follow a small path in the scree marked by occasional cairns to the Col du Meitin (2hrs); on the descent of the Glacier de Corbassière keep L to pass to the W and N of Pts 3155.4 and 3007 on the 1:25 000 map (Valsorey to the Panossiere Hut 5 hrs 30 mins). Cross the Col des Otanes and follow the path up the W side of the Lac de Mauvoisin to the Chanrion Hut – at Ecurie de la Lia it is quicker to drop down onto the main track. (7-8 hrs)

Day 5 Chanrion Hut – Vignettes Hut

Both the Otemma Glacier and the Brenay Glacier route as described under the ski section are feasible, the main differences being:

Otemma Route
from the Chanrion Hut do not go through the bed of the gorge, but take either the road which passes Pts 2319 and 2329 (1:25 000 map) or the higher path which passes Pt 2467 (1:25 000 map). Both routes lead onto the Otemma Glacier. (TOTAL hut to hut: 5 hrs)

Brenay Route
from the hut take the path which passes Pt 2624. (TOTAL hut to hut 7 hrs 30 mins-9hrs)

From the Vignettes Hut it is easy to descend to Arolla for bed, shower and good meal, going up to the Bertol hut the next day.

Day 6 Vignettes Hut – Col de L'Evêque – Bertol Hut

From the hut go W along the ridge to the Col des Vignettes, then S to the rock gap/col a few metres W of Pt 3162m. (1:25 000 map). Head S then SE below Petit Mt Collon to take one of two lines up the Mt Collon Glacier depending on the crevasses:

1. head over towards the foot of the ridge running N from the Col de L'Evêque (Pt 3273 on the 1:25 000 map) and then up to the col, or, more usually,

2. keep to the R (W) close to Pt 3129 and then towards the Col du Petit Mt Collon, before heading L (E) to the Col de L'Evêque 3392m. (1 hr 15 mins).

When descending the upper section of the Haut Arolla Glacier keep to the R (S) at the steep section between 3280-3180m in order to avoid crevasses. Continue N then NW down the Haut Arolla Glacier to c2540m; climb N to pass to the R (E) of Pt 2615.6 to join the main path at the Plans de Bertol Pt 2664. Follow this path NE past Pt 2796 onto the Bertol Glacier. Pass to R (E) of a rock rognon, cross the bergschrund and follow the paint marks on the rocks to the Col de Bertol 3269m. Turn L (N) and a short scramble with fixed ladders leads to the Bertol Hut 3311m. (TOTAL 7hrs)

Day 7 Bertol Hut – Schönbiel Hut

In good weather follow the broad track across the gentle slopes of the upper Mont Miné Glacier towards the Col de la Tête Blanche (between the Tête Blanche and the Col d'Hérens). In poor weather with no track to follow navigation is difficult. Before reaching the col branch off R (S) to climb the Tête Blanche 3724m by its easy snow slopes, descending NE to the col. (3hrs)

It is simple to traverse S round to the Col de Valpelline from which the Tête de Valpelline 3802m can be climbed in 1 hr 15 mins by its straightforward snowslopes.

From the Col de la Tête Blanche or the Col de Valpelline descend NE down the heavily crevassed Stockii Glacier to the Stockii (1hr).

There are now two choices of route:

1. From Pt 3041 descend SE down a small zig-zagging track to Pt 2789 (1:25 000 map). Follow the track E then NE to Pt 2624. Now either: (a) cross the Zmutt Glacier ENE to join the Zermatt path below and to the SE of the hut at c2560m and follow this path back up to the hut; or (b) go N up the Schönbiel Glacier to reach the moraine path at Pt 2738 which is followed down to the hut; or (c) aim for the rock buttress which is to the SSW of the

hut and on its L side find an unlikely but paint-marked track, initially involving very mild rock scrambling and leading straight to the hut. This is the most direct and quick of these three routes. (2 hrs 15 mins) TOTAL 6hrs

2. This is the quicker route in snow conditions and is recommended. From Pt 3041 follow the small track E along the ridge crest to pass under and to the R (S) of Pt 3091.8. A few minutes later you reach a snow saddle from which there descends N a large open snow couloir. Depending on conditions this may be descended on crampons or by a careful glissade. If there is no snow this is loose and unpleasant and not recommended. Cross the dry Schönbiel Glacier N then NE to Pt 2738 where the moraine path is joined and followed briefly SE down to the Schönbiel Hut. (1 hr 15 mins) TOTAL 5hrs

Purists, the impoverished and late arrivals will enjoy the path down to Zermatt through the pine woods and first summer flowers

Day 8 Schönbiel Hut – Zermatt

A well marked path goes down the L moraine of the Zmutt Glacier, down to Zmutt 1936m and on to Zermatt (2 hrs 30 mins-3hrs). It is of course feasible to go direct from the Bertol Hut to Zermatt in one day by not staying at the Schönbiel Hut, and this will suit many parties. If time permits, however, it is worthwhile splitting it into 2 days as the views from the Schönbiel Hut are some of the best in the Alps and you will greatly enjoy the walk down to Zermatt in the early morning as opposed to a weary afternoon slog.

Alternative Start. Argentière – Grands Montets – Trient Hut

The Classic Ski Route of the Col du Chardonnet should only be done when there is plenty of snow, i.e. early in the season. Later in the season the descent of the N side of the Col du Chardonnet may be too loose and unpleasant.

Take the first cablecar at about 0630 (check the times with the Grands Montets Lift Company the day before – see telephone list) and follow the ski route down onto the Argentière Glacier. The ascent of the Chardonnet Glacier starts steeply with some scree and continues steeply up the glacier keeping to the right of centre, crossing to the centre at c2820m to pass through some crevasses. The angle eases now and the route continues without difficulty to the Col du Chardonnet 3323m. (3 hrs 30 mins from Grands Montets)

The N side of the Col du Chardonnet is steep snow and it usual to rope down it – 2 rope lengths being needed to clear the bergschrund in one from a block belay at the top, or there are pegs in place on the L wall if an intermediate belay is required. The best bridge over the bergshcrund is usually on the L as you descend.

Cross the top of the Saleina Glacier NE to pass just below Pt 3091 at which point the Fenêtre de Saleina 3261m becomes visible. The last 30m of this col are steep (1 hr 30 mins). Cross the Plateau du Trient NE then NNE to the Trient Hut. (1 hr 30 mins) TOTAL 6-7 hrs

Walking: Trient Hut –
La Fouly – Bourg St Pierre

This alternative avoids the road section between Champex and Bourg St Pierre and when combined with the Classic Route offers the purist traverse between Chamonix and Zermatt.

Day 1 Trient – La Fouly

From the hut walk down to the Col d'Orny 3098m then E down the Glacier d'Orny to the Cabane d'Orny. Continue E to the Lac d'Orny, then take the path SE to descend steeply down the Vallon d'Arpette de Saleina to Pt 1561. Cross the stream (Reuse de Saleina) to pick up the Tour de Mont Blanc path which goes up the R (W) side of the Drance de Ferret to La Fouly 1593m. TOTAL 4 hrs 30 mins

If you continue to Ferret it saves the La Foule-Ferret walk in the morning.

Day 2 La Fouly – Col des Planards – Bourg St Pierre

Follow the road SE to Ferret and on to Les Ars Dessous, then the path to Les Ars Dessous 1955m. Climb steeply E up a zig-zagging path to the Col des Planards 2737m (as shown on the 1:50 000 map, but on the 1:25 000 it is shown as the Col Sud des Planards 2732m (4 hrs)

From the col descend straight down through rocks – scrambling, no path as such but red marks on the rocks – to meet the path just W of Pt 2515 and the little lake; or descend N then NE to Lake Gouille du Dragon. The N down through rocks (track) to pick up the path which goes down the L (W) side of the Combe des Planards to La Letta 1907m. Either cross the dam to pick up the main road, or stay on the path which turns into a minor road, or stay on the path which turns into a minor road and leads to Bourg St Pierre 1632m. (3hrs) TOTAL 8hrs

Walking: Grande Lui Variation

Cabane de Saleina – Grande Lui – La Fouly

The crossing of the Col de Saleina is more serious than any of the other suggested routes as its N side is 48 degrees for c200m. Good snow cover (more likely early in the season rather than later) and steadiness on crampons are required for this slope.

The Cabane de Saleina can be reached from:

1. The Col du Chardonnet. After descending the N side of the col turn R (E) down the Saleina Glacier, normally passing to the S of Pt 2944. Come off the glacier at c2600m and follow the path up the hut 2691m.

2. The Trient Hut. Cross the Col Droit (also known as the Col des Plines) between Pts 3294 and 3325 on the N ridge of the Aiguilles Dorées. The col is deceptively closer to Pt 3294 than to Pt 3325 and early in the season may have a large cornice. Descend snow and scree to the Glacier des Plines and on down to the Saleina Glacier. Cross this glacier to its R (E) side; descend it to c2600m and follow the path up to the hut 2691m.

3. The Col du Tour. From the Albert Premier Hut cross the Col du Tour (or the Col Superior du Tour if doing the Aiguille du Tour); cross the Plateau du Trient to the Fenêtre de Saleina and descend its steep (but short) S side, head SE downthe Saleina Glacier, passing to theL (N) of Pt 2944.3; continue down the glacier to c2600m and follow the path up to the hut 2691m.

For the crossing of the Col de Saleina and the descent to the A'Neuve Hut follow the ski route (Skiing: Grande Lui Variation). At the A'Neuve Hut pick up the path down to La Fouly.

The Saleina Hut – A'Neuve Hut connection avoiding the Col de Saleina can be made via the Col des Planereuses (again, see Skiing: The Grande Lui Variation).

Walking: Champex – Mauvoisin – Chanrion Hut

Take a taxi or bus to Mauvoisin (simple hotel with overnight accommodation), where there is a choice of route – up the E side of the Lac de Mauvoisin or up the W side. Before the dam was built in 1964 the way up to the hut was up the valley floor along a mule path. The construction company which built the dam also built the road on the W side. Part of the road is tunnelled, and this offers the quickest route to the hut, but the other routes are more pleasant. Cows are brought up to Chanrion by this route for the summer pastures, and the word 'Tse' (which appears frequently on the map of this area) means 'where the cows sleep'. The cows spend a few days at each pasture, reaching the Chanrion Hut about 1st August, then going on up towards the Fenêtre de Durand, before returning by the same route to Fionnay.

This area is rich in wildlife. The first Wildlife Reserve in Switzerland was created here on the Grand Combin in 1886 and in 1968 the Nature Reserve of the Haut Val de Bagnes was formed.

1. E side. Cross the top of the dam or go through a 500m long tunnel which passes right through the dam (slightly claustrophobic) depending on the maintenance currently in progress. The way is clearly signed Chanrion/Giétro/Col de Tsofeiret. Follow the good path along the lake to Ecurie du Giétro 2181m from where it slowly rises to Pt 2642.3 to the SSW of Lac de Tsofeiret. There is a steep section here with a fixed chain, but the path is good and there is no difficulty. Continue S through the Tse des Videttes to the Chanrion hut 2462m. (3 hrs 30 mins from Mauvoison)

2. Road on W side. It is possible to drive a jeep all the way to the Chanrion hut, so this rough road offers the easiest and quickest way. (3hrs)

3. W side path. Follow the road through the tunnel and onto just before Pt

2115. The path now branches off R up the hillside through amazing scenery and guaranteed sightings of bouquetins and edelweiss. It passes through La Tsèsette and then descends to join the jeep tract at the Le Lancet bridge 2040m Follow this easily to the hut. (4 hrs-4hrs 30 mins)

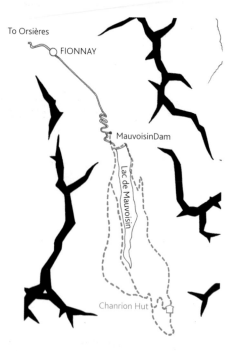

Champex – Mauvoisin – Chanrion Hut

Walking: Chanrion Hut –Dix Hut – Pigne D'Arolla – Vignettes Hut

This variation is well worthwhile, in summer as well as in winter. The summer route follows the ski route, crossing the Col de Lire Rose, Col du Mont Rouge and Col de Cheilon to the Dix Hut; then traversing Pigne d'Arolla to the Vignettes Hut.

Day 1 Chanrion Hut – Dix Hut

From the Chanrion Hut take the path past Pt 2522 to Pt 2624. Continue NE for a while and then cross moraine and glacier ice to the other (N) side. Cross the lateral moraine and climb N towards the Col, passing to the R (E) of the lakes at Pt 2721 and passing to the L (W) of Pt 2756. Pick up a track which leads to the Col de Lire Rose 3115m. (2hrs 30 mins)

Traverse NNE into the bowl of the Lire Rose glacier, and then climb steeply with some loose scree and rock up to the Col du Mont Rouge 3325m. Early in the season there may be steep snow here, which can best be avoided on the L (W). (30 mins)

Traverse NE across the flat upper section of the Gietro glacier to reach the Col de Cheilon. Although this is almost flat, there are some rather unpredictable crevasses causing at least one serious accident in recent years. (30 mins)

Go NE down the easy slopes of the upper cheilon glacier, passing to the L(W) of Pt 2986 – the Swiss 1:50 000 shows the route incorrectly passing to the R (E) of this point. A short traverse and ascent leads to the Dix Hut 2928m. (1hr: TOTAL 5-6 hrs)

Mt Blanc de Cheilon 3869m can be climbed on the way by the WNW Flank (F+/PD) and is well worthwhile for strong parties although it will more likely be done in a separate day from the Dix Hut. See Chapter: Mountains.

Day 2 Dix Hut – Pigne D'Arolla – Vignettes Hut

Go down from the Dix Hut onto the dry Cheilon Glacier and cross it to the de

Tsean Réfien Glacier. Climb up this on the lefthand side, passing through crevasses at c3200m and staying close to the R (W) of Pt 3423. The way ahead looks improbable: continue SW towards the Col de la Serpentine; at 3500m turn L (E) and contour into below a steep slope – the bit which looks improbable. Climb this in a steep rising traverse from R to L (often icy). Gentle slopes lead SE to the Col de Brenay 3639m then ENE to the Pigne d'Arolla Col (3 hrs 30 mins)

Pigne D'Arolla 3796m is well worthwhile for the superb views

The summit of Pigne d'Arolla 3796m can be reached easily in a further 15 minutes. The descent of the Upper Vuibe Glacier to the Vignettes Hut is a straightforward affair in good weather as there will be a wide track to follow. But in bad weather route finding through the numerous crevasses can be difficult. At 3300m there is a choice of route:

1. The direct route turns L and makes a steep and exposed traverse NNE below seracs to the Col des Vignettes. There is danger of falling ice from these seracs, conditions underfoot will invariably be icy and since the route seems to be getting steeper and more serious each year it may be that in time it becomes impracticable. (1hr) TOTAL 5 hrs 30 mins via Pigne d'Arolla

2. An easier but longer option is to descend S from about 3350m down to 3140m then turn L (E) to traverse NE below rocks and then up (steep at one point) to reach the rocky gap/col a few metres W of Pt 3162m (1:25 000 map). Traverse N to the Col des Vignettes, then E to the Hut (30 mins longer).

Walking: Verbier Start

Day 1 Verbier – Mont Fort Hut

Reach the hut very easily using any combination of lifts, roads and paths.

Day 2 Mont Fort Hut – Rosablanche – Prafleuri Hut

Follow the road SE towards Pt 2712 and continue SE up the L (N) side of the Glacier de la Chaux, following a vague track, to the Col de la Chaux 2940m. (2hrs)

Continue SE along a well cairned and marked track to Pt 2982 and then follow the low relief moraine ridge to the small lake Pt 2764. This lake is not visible until you are about 10m from it. (30 mins)

From the S end of the lake cross to the Grand Desert by either the Col de Louvie or the Col de Momin 3003. (1hr). Climb the gentle glacier slopes of the Grand Desert with some large crevasses later in the season to the final easy ridge of the Rosablanche 3336m. (2hrs) Hut to summit 5hrs 30 mins-6hrs

From the summit descend NE then N to pass to the R (E) of Pt 3220 and continue down the L (W) side of the Prafleuri Glacier. Do not attempt to descend the R (E) side direct to the hut. Pick up a track which leads down to the Prafleuri Hut 2624m. (2hrs) TOTAL 8-8 hrs 30 mins

Day 3 Prafleuri Hut – Dix Hut

Take the path over the Col des Roux 2804m (30 mins)

Descend S (good path and cairns which get slightly lost in the rocks) to the chalets of La Barma 2458m and continue SSE along the path by the side of the Lac des Dix. At the end of the lake at Pt 2386 there is an awkward rock step (the Pas du Chat). Follow the track SE then S up the moraine to the Dix Hut. (3hrs 30 mins - 4hrs) TOTAL 4hrs - 4 hrs 30 mins

Walking: Zermatt – Saas Fee

There are two suggested routes, the longer one over the Adler Pass giving the option of a 4000m peak (the Strahlorn 4190m) and a shorter way over the Alphubeljoch, also giving the option of a 4000m peak (the Alphubel 4206m).

Route 1 Zermatt – Fluhalp Hut – Adler Pass – Saas Fee

Day 1 Zermatt – Fluhulp Hut
Take the lift systems to Sunnegga 2289m and Blauherd 2581m. Follow the path E, starting with a short descent, past the Stellisee to the Fluhalp Hut (part of the hotel) 2616m. (45 mins)

Day 2 Fluhulp Hut – Adler Pass – Britannia Hut
Follow a good path E across rocks then a level plain to a fork near a small lake (15 mins). Take the R track which goes along the crest of a lateral moraine and then either (1) go down to the Findeln Glacier at 2780m or (2) continue along the moraine and rocks, getting onto the glacier at c2850m.

Continue E to the foot of the Adler Glacier which is steep and crevassed. At this point the glacier is usually half dry and half covered with snow, and finding a way through the junction can be tricky. Keep close to the L (N) using the scree slopes above before joining the higher snowfield. Go E then NE up the Adler Glacier to the Adler Pass. The final snow slope may be icy. (4 hrs-4 hrs 30 mins)

The Strahlhorn 4190m can be easily climbed by its WNW Ride (1hr).

Go N then NNE down the easy angled slopes of the Allalin Glacier. At c 3460m move R towards the middle of the glacier to get the best line through crevasses. Continue NE down gentle slopes past Pt 3258 to pass close by Pt 3143.3. Cross the Hohlaub Glacier NE and follow the track up to the Britannia Hut 3029m. (2hrs) TOTAL 8 hrs 30 mins -9hrs 30 mins

Day 3 Britannia Hut– Saas Fee
The quickest descent is by following the wide track WNW to the Felskinn Lift; but a pleasant and slightly longer way is to descend the Kessjen Glacier N to pick up a good path which traverses the E flank of the Egginer, to bring you, with a

few small ups and downs, to the top of the Plattjen Lift 2559.9m and so down to Saas Fee.

Route 2 Zermatt – Täsch Hut – Alphubeljoch – Saas Fee

Day 1 Zermatt – Täsch Hut

There are two ways:

1. walk down the road towards Täsch as far as Pt 1524.8 from where a pleasant shaded path rises NE through the woods to join the main Täsch-Täsch Hut path at 2000m Follow this to Ottavan and continue on the upper path to the Täsch Hut 2708m (5hrs).

2. take the train down to Täsch and follow the path to the hut (4hrs from Täsch).

Day 2 Täsch Hut – Alphubeljoch – Saas Fee

Ascend E past Pt 3052 to the Alphubel Glacier and continue E to the Alphubeljoch 3782m (2hrs – 2hrs 30 mins)

Go NE then diagonally N down the glacier to c3400m where the main Langfluh-Alphubel track may be met. Continue basically NE straight down the glacier to Langfluh with suitable detours to avoid the numerous crevasses. One way of avoiding the lower crevasses is to cut R (SE) at 3180m and pass through the snowy crevassed gap between the rock ridge and Pt 3173.7. This leads to easy ground and the summer ski piste down to Langfluh. (2hrs) TOTAL 4hrs 30 mins-5hrs

If climbing the Alphubel, make a rising traverse NW from the Alphubeljoch to 3900m. Continue NW up the steep slope ahead (crevasses), turning L (W) at 4100m to the summit the Alphubel 4206m. (1 hr 30 mins; 4 hrs 30 mins from the Täsch Hut). The descent is E down to the foot of the steep section at 3900m, then NE down the glacier to 3400 and on down to Langfluh (2 hrs 30 mins) TOTAL Täsch Hut-Alphubel-Langfluh 7 hrs 30 mins.

From Langfluh take the lift down to Saas Fee.

Italian High Level Route

The route starts at the Klein Matterhorn Lift and traverses the Swiss/Italian frontier ridge, staying mostly on the Italian side until Monte Rosa and then dropping down to the Monte Rosa Hut and back to Zermatt. There are opportunities to climb: the Breithorn, Pollux, Castor, Liskamm, Piramide Vincent, Ludwigshöhe, Parrot Spitze, Signalkuppe, Zumstein Spitze and the Dufourspitze – a fair handful of 4,000m peaks.

The summer route varies in Grade between PD and AD depending on which of these mountains are taken in. If Liskamm and the traverse of the Dufourspitze are included, the Grade is AD. Few ski mountaineers will undertake these routes as the problem of carrying skis on delicate technical ground outweighs any subsequent ski descents. Also, in the ski mountaineering season there is the added problem of unconsolidated cornices and avalanches. So the ski mountaineering route takes the earliest line, while the summer route can be varied.

The route can be split at will by using the following Italian huts: Ayas, Mezzalama, Quintino Sella, Gnifetti, Mantova and Margherita. As with all huts it is recommended to make reservations by telephone, but in the case of these huts it is particularly important in the ski mountaineering season to check that the guardian will be there. If the guardian is not there, the hut will be open but you will have to carry food.

The route never drops below 3500m and the route finding can be difficult with heavily crevassed glaciers, so a period of settled weather is definitely required.

Zermatt or Cervinia are useful starting points.

Summer (Walking Route)
Day 1. Zermatt – Breithorn – Ayas Hut

From the top of the Klein Matterhorn Lift the Breithorn 4165m. is one of the

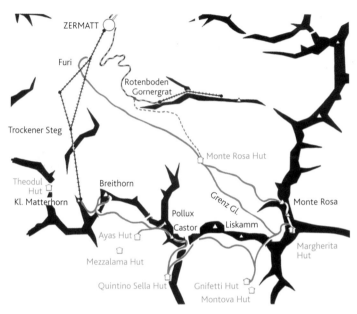

Italian High Level Route

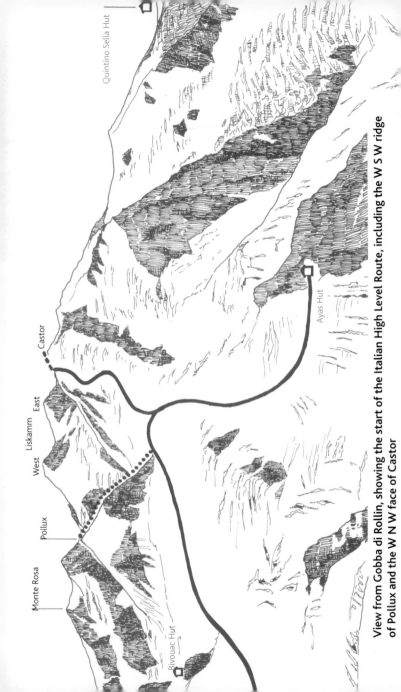

View from Gobba di Rollin, showing the start of the Italian High Level Route, including the W S W ridge of Pollux and the W N W face of Castor

easiest 4,000m peaks in the Alps. It is climbed by its S Face, usually by making a steep rising traverse L across the face (bergschrund) to come in just W of the summit 4165m. (1 hr 30 mins)

From the summit descend the snow ridge ESE towards Pt 4081, then turn R (SSW) down towards the Breithorn Pass. Cross the Verra Grande Glacier E to pass just above Pt 3675 (1:50,000 map), i.e. just below the Rossi e Volante Bivouac Hut on the 1:25,000. Descend slightly (bad crevasses); then climb SE towards the foot of the WSW Ridge of Pollux. When just past the foot of the ridge, i.e. SE of it, at c.3730m, turn sharply R to head S then back W, to pass through crevasses and then more easily S to the hut, 3420m. The direct route S from the Rossi Bivouac Hut is not normally possible in summer due to crevasses. If visibility is bad and if the wind has blown in the track, route finding on this section can be very difficult. (3 hrs) TOTAL 4 hrs mins

Day 2. Ayas Hut – Pollux – Castor – Quintino Sella Hut

Pollux and Castor are the Zwillinge (the Twins) and on this route are traversed West-East at PD+. Pollux is normally climbed by its WSW Ridge, and may be descended by its SE Ridge to the Zwillingsjoch. However if it is bare of snow the SE Ridge may be loose and unpleasant; and most parties therefore choose to climb back down the WSW Ridge, which means that packs can be left at its foot.

From the hut head back up the glacier to the foot of the WSW Ridge of Pollux, where packs can be left. The ridge can either be started on its R (SE) side where a vague track finds its way up loose rocks, or it can be started up the L (NW) side, where there tends to be more snow and less loose rock. Stay on the ridge crest with one move out onto the R (SE) side; there is then a section of Grade 3 with fixed ropes, following by the final snow arête. (2 hrs 30 mins)

Descend by the same route to the foot of the ridge (1 hr), or in good snow descend the SE Ridge to the Zwillingsjoch.

Climb Castor by its WNW snow slope. Near the top there is a bergschrund followed by a short steep snow/ice step, and then the final narrow and exposed snow arête to the summit or, avoid the bergschrund by a rising traverse R across the face; or go out L before the bergschrund and up a steepish snow slope to gain the ridge on the L. (1 hr 30 mins)

Descend the SE Ridge of Castor over 2 small humps, snow all the way, to the Felikjoch (15 mins). The direct descent from the Felikjoch is very steep, so start by climbing a few metres E, then turn R (ESE) down a snow ridge, then R (SW) down the glacier to the Quintino Sella Hut 3585m. (45 mins) TOTAL 7 hrs 30 mins

Italian High Level Route: the Signalkuppe and Margherita Hut, with the Parrot Spitze on the right

This hut can be reached in one day from Zermatt by leaving out the Ayas Hut and Pollux, but still traversing Castor.

The descent in bad weather from the Quintino Sella Hut to Staffa/Gressoney is: Head S to an exposed ridge and fixed ropes. At 3490m turn SW down more open ground with scree and loose rocks (paint markings and cairns are scarce and this section can be difficult in poor visibility and/or snow). The track and paint markings become much more obvious. Head S to Passo di Bettolini; then on the L (E) side of the ridge to the lift station which is just above and to the NE of Col di Bettaforcla 2672m.

Day 3 Quintello Sella Hut – Passo del Naso – Margherita Hut

From the Quintino Sella Hut across the Felik Glazier NE to pass above Pt 3744. Continue NE then E across the Lis Glacier, keeping above some large crevasses, to the foot of a snow dome called the Naso 4272m. Climb the steep W flank of this snow dome (40 degrees, which can be exposed and serious if icy) to gain the so-called Passo del Naso c.4100m on its S side. This is not a col as such but the easiest way through. (2 hrs 30 mins)

From the Passo, either 1. descend a steep slope to the E (50 degrees for 100m) – expect anything from soft snow, to ice and loose rocks; or 2. turn down R (S), usually marker posts to a snow slope which is descended to c.3920m; then turn

View east from the Passo del Naso

Balmenhorn Hut

4321

Ludwigshöhe

4341

Parrot Spz.

Signalkuppe and Margherita Hut

L (E then NE) below rocks to come in below the steep slope of route (1).

Contour round at the 4000m level below a large icefall, then bear L (NE) to cross the frontier ridge just R (SE) of Pt 4260, well to the R (E) of the Lisjoch. (2 hrs)

Traverse NE at c.4230m below the Parror Spitze (track in good weather), bearing L (N then NW) to pass at a safe distance below an icefall; then back R (N then NE) to flat ground just S of the Colle Gnifetti. The final slopes up to the Margherita Hut 4556m. May be icy. (1 hr 45 mins) TOTAL 6 hrs

The Margherita Hut is built on the summit of the Signalkuppe, one of the three summits on Monte Rosa. It is the highest hut in the Alps and overnight stays are usually associated with feeling sick, eating little and having a headache. If you do sleep, which is unlikely, bad dreams and nightmares are usual.

Variation 1 Liskamm E Peak by the Ridge (Cresta Sella).
From the top of the El Naso snow dome descend N to a col, the Colle della Fronte 4239m. A snow arête leads onto the rock ridge, which is climbed on the crest all the way except when turning a few small gendarmes, joining the E Ridge 15 mins. from the summit 4527m. AD. 6 hrs from the Quintino Sella Hut

Descend the E Ridge to the Lisjoch. This starts with rocks, but soon becomes snow. Some of it is steep and exposed, and movements have to be made onto the N Face to avoid the cornices which invariably hang over the S side and which can be enormous. (PD; 1 hr).

Variation 2 Traverse of Liskamm W and E Peaks
From the Quintino Sella Hut retrace the descent route to the Felikjoch. Climb the Frontier SW Ridge, which is a snow ridge all the way. At 4214m there is a hump which is turned on the L (Swiss) side; then a steepish rising traverse – exposed. (PD; 4 hrs, hut to W Peak).

The ridge between the two summits is long (1 kilometre), often corniced on the S requiring movements out onto the Swiss side above the N Face. Soon after leaving the W Peak, descend rocks which are steep and exposed. Thereafter in goods conditions follow the track (narrow – very) to the E Summit. (AD; 1 hr 15 mins-2 hrs).

Descend the SE Ridge of the E Summit to the Lisjoch (description above; PD, 45 mins-1 hr).

Join the normal route to the Margherita Hut (2 hrs) TOTAL 8-9 hrs. Or drop down to the Gnifetti or Mantova Huts (45 mins).

Italian High Level Route: between the Lisjoch and the Signalkuppe the track passes close beneath the ice-cliffs of the Parrot Spitze

Variation 3 Gnifetti and Mantova Huts.

The Gnifetti Hut lies to the S of the Lisjoch at 3611m and the Mantova Hut is immediately below the Gnifetti Hut at 3460m on the other side of the glacier.

Both involve a drop of height which will have to be regained the next day. They nevertheless offer a good bolt hole if the weather is poor or they can be used in their own right to climb a good selection of 4000m peaks – Piramide Vincent 4215m. Lugwigshöhe 4341m and Parrot Spitze 4436m, (an airy and highly recommended traverse). Cross the frontier ridge between Pt 4260 and the Ludwigshöhe, and go on to the Margherita Hut.

Day 4. Margherita Hut – Dufourspitze – Monte Rosa Hut

It is possible to descend the Grenz Glacier to the Monte Rosa Hut following the ski route; but in summer the crevasses can be difficult. If in condition there will be a well beaten track down the Grenz Glacier, taking the N Route past Pts 4027 and 3696.

However, one of the most spectacular easy routes in the Alps is to traverse the Dufourspitze, up by the SE Ridge (AD) and down by the W Ridge (PD).

From the Margherita Hut descend to the Colle Gnifetti 4454m, then climb an easy snow slope followed by rocks to the Zumstein Spitze 4563m. (30 mins)

Descend the N Ridge of the Zumsten Spitze – a steep snow ridge with one rock step – to the Grenzsattel 4452m. Climb the SE Ridge of the Dufourspitze, starting on the L of the ridge, then moving back onto the ridge itself. Traverse broken rocks on the L, finishing on good rocks to the Grenzgipfel 4596m. (Grade 2). The exposed ridge to the Dufourspitze 4634m has one down move, tricky if icy. (Grade 3) (AD) (2 hrs 15 mins)

Descend the W Ridge of the Dufourspitze (PD) which starts with a chimney, then easy rocks, followed by a snow couloir on the R which can be icy and exposed. Further easy rocks lead onto the final snow ridge down to the Sattel 4359m. (1 hr)

Turn R and go NW down the Monte Rosa Glacier, curving R then back L to avoid crevasses at c4060m. Pass fairly close to Pt 3827 and the rock ridge running down from it. At c3500m turn L (W) to reach a crevassed area. The way through this can be difficult to find but trends R to reach the snow between Pts 3277.3 and 3303. Continue down this snow, maybe bare glacier ice, to the Ob. Plattje. Keep on NW down this broad rock spur through tiresome boulders with a choice of several tracks, picking up a more definite path at c300m which leads down to the Monte Rosa Hut 2795m. (3 hrs) TOTAL 7 hrs 30 mins-8 hrs

Day 5. Monte Rosa Hut – Zermatt

From the hut a path leads down onto the glacier. Cross this NNW to Pt 2657 (1:25,000 map) which is just R (E) of Pt 2678. Take the good path up to Rotenboden and then the Gornergrat train down to Zermatt.

Ski Mountaineering Route

The best time to ski the route is between mid-May and early-June, when the days are long and the weather usually settled. Later in June the crevasses on the Genz Glacier may be troublesome.

The main differences from the Summer Route are:

Day 1 to the Ayas Hut.

When you are just below the Rossi e Volante Bivouac Hut turn R and ski down S through crevasses, turn L (E) to pass below an icefall, and so down to the hut. This is a direct and quick route, normally impassable in summer due to the crevasses.

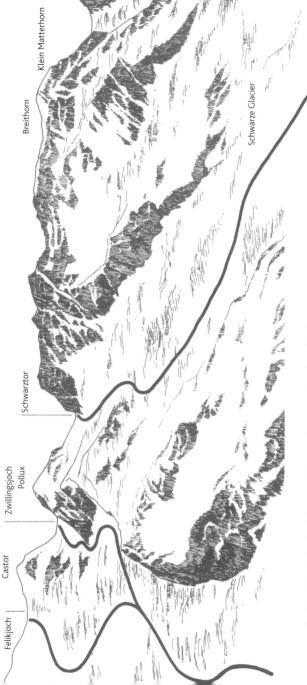

The N. side of the Breithorn, Pollux and castor showing the descents from the Scharztor Zwillingsjoch and Felikjoch

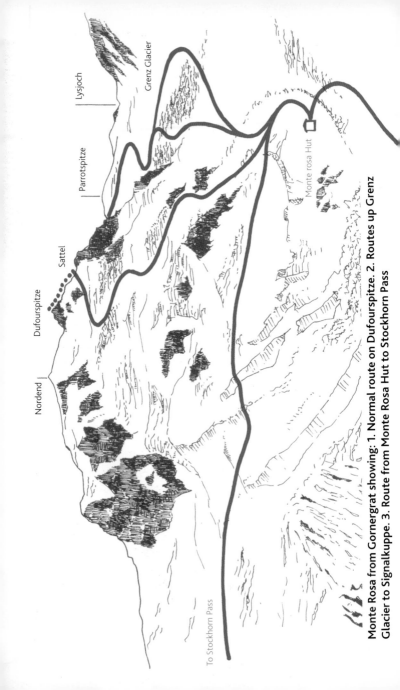

Monte Rosa from Gornergrat showing: 1. Normal route on Dufourspitze. 2. Routes up Grenz Glacier to Signalkuppe. 3. Route from Monte Rosa Hut to Stockhorn Pass

Day 2 Ayas Hut to Quintino Sella Hut.

The traverse of Castor may be too serious, particularly if icy. A straightforward and recommended alternative is via the Castor Glacier and Col Perazzi.

From the Ayas Hut ski W then S down to the Mezzalama Hut; then turn L (NE) onto the Piccolo Vera Glacier. On skins climb SE to gain the R (S) side of the Castor Glacier (unnamed on the Swiss 1:50,000 map); at c2400m come back towards the middle of the glacier and continue to the Col Perazzi (unnamed on the Swiss 1:50,000 but 3860m NE of Punta Perazzi 3906). To climb Castor continue ENE towards the Felikjoch which is gained by its ESE ridge (leave skis as soon as the ridge steepens), and then follow the SE Ridge of Castor to its summit. To reach the Quintino Sella Hut from the Col Perazzi ski S down straightforward glacier slopes.

Day 3 Choice between Margherita Hut and Gnifetti Hut.

In the ski mountaineering season it is unlikely that the guardian will be resident at the Margherita Hut and the prospect of a cold and sleepless night in the winter room deters all but the most hardy. In any case the main reason for staying in the Margherita Hut is to get an early start on the traverse of the Dufourspitze, and this is not a ski mountaineering route. A far more attractive proposition is to use the Gnifetti Hut, the descent to which is straightforward and normally well tracked. For such a large hut it is well concealed when approached from the N, and in bad weather it is advisable to pick up the E end of the rock ridge on which the hut is built and then go W along the N side of the ridge.

Piramide Vincent 4215m can be climbed by its easy N flank either on the way down to the Gnifetti Hut or the next morning on the way back up.

Day 4 Signalkuppe and descent of the Grenz Glacier.

From the Gnifetti Hut skin back N up the glacier to cross the frontier ridge just R (SE) of Pt 4260 and follow the summer route to the Signalkuppe 4556m. (3 hrs)

Descent of the Grenz Glacier. In the ski mountaineering season this is a heavily crevassed glacier, requiring careful route finding, but at the same time offering a direct descent to the Monte Rosa Hut with superb skiing in a very high Alpine environment. In poor weather and without tracks it is a very serious undertaking.

Between c.3940-3740m there is a heavily crevassed area. There are two routes: (1) the normal route is to head W then across R (NNW) to the top of a slope at c3960m which takes you down NW with badly crevassed areas on either side. This brings you close to the bottom of the SW Ridge of the Dufourspitze (Pt 3753 on the 1:25,000 map).

Alternatively (2) head L (W) across the glacier to ski down right under the N Face of Liskamm – subsequent risk from avalanches coming down the face.

The next obstacle is the icefall between c3600-3400m, which can be avoided by two routes: (1) Continue NW down easy slopes to pass through the narrow gap between Pt 3699 and the rocks to the N of it. Carry on down NW with crevasses and seracs on your L and the rock ridge on your R until level with the bottom of the rock ridge Pt 3472. (2) Instead of passing through the narrow gap at Pt 3699 head L (W) across the glacier to pass round the other side of the icefall.

Easier ground with fewer crevasses brings you NW then NNW to the Ob Plattje at Pt 3109. Easy skiing down the snow covered slopes of the rocky Plattje brings you to the Monte Rosa Hut.

Day 5 Monte Rosa Hut to Zermatt.

Very late in the ski mountaineering season it may be possible to use the summer route across to Rotenboden, but this is normally inadvisable due to the avalanche risk when traversing below the Gornergrat. The usual route is to ski down the Gorner Glacier.

For most of the way this is very easy and the line you take will probably be dictated by old climbing tracks which will give you fast schusses to carry you over the bumps and flat areas. At c2500m head across R (N) to pass down the R side of the glacier, and then you come to the snout of the glacier.

This is steep and later in the season may be icy in which case crampons will be need. Being surrounded by high rocks adds to the atmosphere. A line close to the rocks on the R (NE) may be possible; but often the best line is to come back to the L (SW) at c2320m and descend the steep section with a series of diagonal side slips.

If there is enough snow ski on down to Pt 1939 (Pt 1945 on the 1:25,000). Cross the bridge and traverse out onto the slopes on the L, to join the ski run from Schwarzee to Furi 1864m. Alternatively take a higher line on the L, passing just above Pt 2190 (Pt 2193 on the 1:25,000), and follow the line of the summer path to join the same ski run. From Furi take the lift down to Zermatt.

If there is little snow at the foot of the glacier snout, pick up the path at Pt 2005 on the 1:25,000. This goes down the R side of the Gornera stream. At 1829m. there is a fork – the L going over the bridge to Furi (which is worth taking if the lifts are still running), the R going on down to Winkelmatten and Zermatt.

Mountains

Monte Rosa

Monte Rosa is the highest mountain in Switzerland and has three summits – Dufourspitze 4618m, Nordend 4609m, and the Signalkuppe 4556m. Despite its steepness the Monte Rosa Glacier is relatively crevasse free and because it faces NW it nearly always has good snow conditions, Although not technically difficult, these peaks will only be successfully realised by those who are fit and acclimatised.

At dawn the shadow of Mt Blanc lies across the vale of Geneva

The normal summer route is the Dufourspitze via the W Ridge. Ski mountaineers will either do this route or the Signalkuppe via the Grenz Glacier. Both of these are described in descent in the chapter on the Italian High Level Route, as is the traverse from the Signalkuppe to the Dufourspitze – a classic summer expedition.

Mont Blanc *4808m*

It is usually difficult to combine an ascent of Mont Blanc with the Haute Route – time, money and tiredness prevailing. So the ascent of the highest mountain in the Pennine Alps is usually undertaken as a separate enterprise. It is technically easy but makes

Mont Blanc, showing the Grands Mulets route and part of the Goûter Route

Aig. du Midi

Mt. Maudit

Mt Blanc du Tacul

MONT BLANC

Dôme de Goûter

Goûter Hut

Vallot Hut

Gr. Mulets Hut

Plan de L'Aiguille

CHAMONIX

Mont Blanc – Vallée Blanche

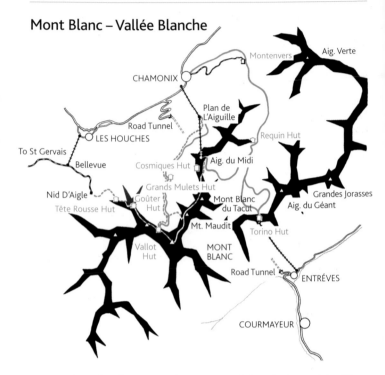

enormous demands on fitness and acclimatisation. Settled weather is essential, as Mont Blanc is a mountain notorious for low temperatures and strong winds.

Route 1 The Goûter Route

The normal summer route and the easiest way up the mountain, although the objective danger of rockfall in the Grand Couloir is out of proportion to the rest of the route. The Goûter Hut is extremely busy – it is normal for there to be 3 people to 2 mattresses. Grade PD-.

Day 1. Les Houches – Goûter Hut

Take the cablecar from Les Houches to Bellevue, then the train to Nid d'Aigle 2386m. A good path climbs NE then E to the foot of the rock ridge coming NW down from the Tête Rousse Hut. The path winds steeply up this ridge to the small glacier level with the Tête Rousse Hut (2 hrs). Cross this glacier being careful of stonefall to reach the L (N) side of the Grand Couloir. Great care is required in crossing this Couloir due to the frequent stonefalls which come down it. The size of some of the rocks which come down and the speed at which they move can make this a very dangerous place. A wire is sometimes stretched across it and this may be clipped for security, although many opt to ignore the wire in favour of extra speed. Cross fast watching above all the time. Follow the track up the ridge on the far side of the Couloir with some easy scrambling and fixed ropes, to the Goûter Hut 3817m. It is worthwhile to wear helmets for the crossing of the Couloir and this ridge. Even the ridge is not entirely safe, as bad rockfalls down the Grand Couloir can result in rocks bouncing up and going over the ridge, so it is essential to always be on your guard. (2 hrs) TOTAL Nid d'Aigle to Goûter Hut 4 hrs

Day 2. Goûter Hut – Mont Blanc

Leave the hut in the dark, at about 0300 hrs and follow what is usually a well trodden track up the glacier over the Dome du Goûter and up to the Vallot Hut 4362m. (2 hrs) The route follows the frontier ridge SE over the Bosses, quite steep in places. The final snow/ice ridge is exposed and requires care. There is minimum crevasse danger, so it is usual to rope up on a short rope which has the two advantages of being the right length for holding a slip and of being less likely to get in the way of the many other parties who will no doubt be on the route. (2 hrs) TOTAL 4 hrs

Route 2 Traverse of Mont Blanc du Tacul and Mont Maudit.

With the new Cosmiques Hut this route has become more popular as a summer route. It can also be done from the first Midi cablecar (departs at c0615 hrs, which means you get away from the Midi at 0700 and reach the summit at 1400). Or be traditional and bivouac at the site of the old Abri Simond Hut at the foot of the Cosmique Arête. Grade PD.

Cross the Col du Midi and follow the normal route up Mont Blanc du Tacul. In fine weather there will be an obvious trail and you will not be alone, although two large bergschrunds can cause problems, especially in the dark with no track to follow. Leave the actual summit of Mont Blanc di Tacul for another day, and descend easily S to the Col Maudit.

The N side on Mont Maudit progressively steepens and has a bergschrund about three quarters-way up. It is usually best to take this on the L and to then traverse back R above it (delicate and exposed), to make a rising traverse to the Col du Maudit 4345m. Descend S to the Col de las Brenva 4303m.

Climb the Mur de la Côte, quite steep and maybe icy. The final section via the Petis Rochers Rouges and Petits Mulets is less steep, but it takes a lot longer than expected, partly due to tiredness and partly because it is very foreshortened.

(Cosmiques Hut to Mont Blanc: 7 hrs)

Route 3 Grands Mulets Route

This is the normal ski mountaineering route and it may also be a feasible route in summer, both in ascent and descent, but only if the Jonction below the hut is not too crevassed. As the summer goes on, so the crevasses get bigger. Wooden planks are put over some of the worst, but numerous diversions are required and it becomes a dangerous place. Local advice should always be taken before planning to go this way in summer – and a rope should always be worn. Grade PD in summer, but AD for ski mountaineering due to the seriousness of the crevasses in Spring time.

Day 1. Chamonix – Grands Mulets Hut

From the Plan de l'Aiguille (the halfway station of the Midi) climb easily SE to Pt 2385, overlooking the Pélerins Glacier. The summer route crosses the glacier horizontally SW, then follows the path SW past the derelict Gare des Glaciers lift station 2414m. to reach the Bossons Glacier at c.2500m The ski mountaineering route crosses the Pelerins Glacier SSW and higher up to pass below the N Ridge of the Midi at c.2550m; it then turns R (SW) to join the Bossons Glacier at the same place as the summer route.

Follow an obvious terrace SW across the Bossons Glacier, and then turn L (S) to climb up and into the Jonction. This is a confused area of seracs and crevasses, and then the exact route varies according to conditions. Easier slopes lead SSE to the rock island of the Grands Mulets Hut 3051m. (4 hrs-4 hrs 30 mins).

Day 2. Grands Mulets Hut – Mont Blanc

From the hut climb SSW to pass well to the R (W) of Pic Wilson 3266m; bear slightly R (SW) towards the rock island Pt 3330. Leave this on your R, and curve back L (SSW) to pass to the R (W) of Pt 3509 – the Rocher de l'Heureux Retour. A steeper slope leads to the Petite Plateau. Up to this point the main danger has been from crevasses, but now the bigger threat is from the huge ice cliffs high up on the R. Keep as far L (E) as possible to avoid this danger, and another steeper slope (the Grands Montets) brings you to the easier slopes of the Grand Plateau. At c.4000m turn R (SW) and climb up to the Col du Dôme (c.4250m). Cross the bergschrund and head L (SE) up to the Vallot Hut, where skis are normally left and the Goûter route is joined (5-6 hrs.).

The descent on skis by the same route can be very good, and it is normal to get back down to Chamonix on the same day.

Mont Velan *3731m*

Mt Velan is one of the best ski mountain in the Alps, as it has all the character of a high mountain including crevassed glaciers and the crossing of a delicate col. And yet skis are taken to the summit, nowhere does the grade exceed PD and the ski descent is usually superb. A fit party need not lose a day on the Haute Route: go in one day from the Trient Hut to Bourg St. Pierre and on to the Velan Hut, and on the next day climb Mont Velan and then go up to the Valsorey Hut.

Day 1. Bourg St Pierre – Velan Hut

From Bourg St. Pierre follow the Valsorey Hut route as far as the meadow below the Chalet d'Amont. Make a rising traverse R from the meadow, passing above the gorge and Pt 2257, to gain the crest of the moraine which leads up to the hut. The summer route crosses the bridge before the meadow (signposted) and follows the path. (4 hrs)

Day 2 Velan Hut – Mt. Velan – Valsorey Hut

Climb on skins up the moraine and then onto the Tseudet Glacier, keeping to the R (W) side until near Pt 2814. Cross the glacier R to climb a steep slope on the L (E) side and on up to the rocky Col de la Gouille 3150m which has a 50m section of 45 degrees, and which is done on foot. The descent on the other side to the Valsorey Glacier is just as steep. Climb up the glacier, at first on the L and then more in the centre, depending on the crevasses. Keep L to avoid rocks and then turn R (NW) up to the summit (5-6 hrs).

The descent to the Velan Hut is by the same route (2 hrs) TOTAL 8 hrs

From the Velan Hut ski down the Tseudet Glacier to pass to the S and above Pt 2387. Cross the lateral moraine to join the normal route to the Valsorey Hut at the Grands Plans 2501.8.

Mont Blanc de Cheilon *3869m*

The Dix Hut is the usual starting point for the normal route, although it can be climbed en route when traversing from the Chanrion Hut to Dix Hut.

Summer Route

From the Col de Cheilon climb the rocky WNW ridge (F+/PD) until it is possible to move L at c3520m onto a snow slope which leads up to the col at 3785m. (1:25,000 map). This snow slope is steep at one section and may be icy later in the season. Follow the final SW rock ridge to the summit (2 hrs). Descent is by the same route. Grade PD-.

When coming from the Chanrion Hut it may be possible to save time by taking the ski route as far as the col at 3785m. Beware of descending by the ski route unless you are sure it is possible, as large crevasses frequently bar the way later in the season.

Ski Route

From the Col de Cheilon continue SSE across the flat Giétro Glacier until SWS of Pt 3359. If coming from the Chanrion Hut reach this same point from the Col du Mont Rouge.

Turn L (E) and climb through crevasses in a general SE direction to a height of c.3500m If anything keep R (W) during this section in order to avoid seracs on the L. At c3500m bear L in a rising curve, E then NE, up a glacier ramp to pass just to the L (W) of Pt 3827. Continue NE just below the crest of the ridge and then onto the ridge itself at the col at 3785m. The final narrow rock ridge is climbed on foot to the top 3869m, but in winter/spring such a large cornice may form on the R (E) side of this ridge as to make it impracticable, and most parties will be content with the S summit 3827m. (3 hrs from leaving the Giétro glacier). Grade PD.

Descend by the same route.

L'Evêque 3716m.

L'Evêque (Grade PD) is a good ski mountain from the Vignettes Hut. Ski down to the Col de Chermontane 3053m; skin SE, then E through crevasses; and finally SE up to a steeper glacier cwm to the Col de la Mitre 3528m. (Ski depot). Crampons are invariably needed for the final steep slope and rock ridge. (Ascent 3 hrs, descent 2 hrs.)

Mont Gelé, Mont Avril, Pigne D'Arolla, La Luette

Descriptions of routes on these mountains appear in the text, as they are usually undertaken as part of a traverse.

Telephone Numbers

International Codes

Country codes: France 33, Switzerland 41, Italy 39, UK 44.

Dial 00 then the country codes; and then the number, dropping the first 0 of the number; except for numbers in Italy where the first 0 is kept

Valley Bases

(D = dortoir/bunk accommodation available)

Argentière

Gite du Belvedere	D	04 50 54 02 59
Gite La Boerne, Montroc	D	04 50 54 06 03
Hotel La Couronne		04 50 54 00 02
Hotel Le Dahu		04 50 54 01 55

Arolla

Hotel le Glacier	D	0272 83 12 18
Hotel le Sporting	D	0272 83 17 06
Michel Rong-Anzevui	D	0272 83 15 14

Bourg St Pierre

Auberge du Valsorey	D	0277 87 11 76
Auberge du Vieuz-Moulin	D	0277 87 11 69
Auberges Les Charmettes	D	0277 87 11 50
Au Petit Vèlan	D	0277 87 11 41
Hotel du Crêt	D	0277 87 11 43
Hotel/Motel Bivouac Napolèon		0277 87 11 62

Chamonix

Le Chamoniard	D	04 50 53 40 09
La Montagne	D	04 50 53 11 60
Refuge des Amis de la Montagne	D	04 50 53 17 83

Champex

Chalet-Pension 'En Plain Air'	D	0277 83 23 50
Relais au Club Alpin (SAC)	D	0277 83 11 61
Relais au Val d'Arpette	D	0277 83 12 21

The Haute Route

Courmayer
Hotel Svizzero   D   0165 84 20 35

Entrèves/La Palaud
Hotel Funivia   D   0165 89 9 24
Hotel JolyD   0165 89 9 49

Great St Bernard

Monastery   D   0277 87 11 72

La Fouly

Hotel Edelweiss   D   0277 83 26 21
Hotel des Glaciers   D   0277 83 11 71

Mauvoisin
Hotel   0277 7 91 30

Saas Fee
Hotel Bergheimat   0279 57 20 30

Zermatt
Hotel Bahnhof   D   0279 67 24 06
Hotel Rhodania   0279 67 28 63
                                            (North Wall Pizza Restaurant)

Taxis

Andy Cleaver (Chamonix)   04 50 53 63 97
Costa (Argentière)   04 50 54 04 30
Chamonix Bus   04 50 53 05 55
Coquoz (Champez)   0277 31 18 43
Pen (Champez)   0277 36 13 18
Fredy (Zermatt)   0279 67 33 69

Tourist Offices

Argentière   04 50 54 02 14
Arolla   0272 38 11 67
Chamonix   04 50 53 00 24

Courmayeur	0165 84 20 60
La Fouly	0277 42 71 7
Saas Fee	0279 57 14 57
Verbier	0277 31 35 85
Zermatt	0279 66 11 81

Recorded Weather/Avalanche Forecasts

France

Departmental	
(the last 2 digits are the department)	36 68 02 (74)
All France	08 36 68 01 01
Snow/Avalanches	08 36 68 10 20
Internet	www.meteo.fr

Switzerland

General Weather	162
Snow Report	120
Avalanches	187
Special Weather Report	157 126 21
Swiss Alpine Weather	157 126 218
Mont Blanc Area	157 126 23
Internet	www.sma.ch

General

French Alpine Club, Chamonix	04 50 53 16 03
Guides Bureau, Argentière	04 50 54 00 12
Guides Bureau, Chamonix	04 50 53 00 88
Guides Bureau, Saas Fee	0279 57 44 64
Guides Bureau, Zermatt	0279 67 34 56
Maison de la Montagne	04 50 53 22 08
Rescue, Chamonix PGHM	04 50 53 16 89
Rescue, Swiss	117

Lift Companies

Breya, Champex	0277 83 13 44
Gornergrat/Stockhorn	0279 67 27 4
Grands Montets, Argentière	04 50 54 00 8
Le Tour	04 50 54 00 58

Montenvers Railway	04 50 53 12 54
Aiguille du Midi, Chamonix	04 50 53 40 00
Saas Fee	0279 57 14 14
Saas Fee	0279 57 12 72
Super St. Bernard	0277 4 91 10
Verbier	0277 31 61 01
Zermatt	0279 67 23 10

Note

The Grands Montets Lift is closed between 15th and 30th May approx. each year. The Argentière Hut closes on about the same date, re-opening at the end of June.

Huts

A'Neuve	0277 83 24 24
Albert Premier	04 50 54 06 20
Argentière	04 50 53 16 92
Ayas	0125 30 80 83
Bertol	0272 83 19 29
Bouquetins (home no.)	021 85 63 21
Britannia	0279 57 22 88
Chanrion	0277 78 12 09
Dix	0272 81 15 23
D'Orny	0277 83 18 87
Fluhalp	0279 67 25 51
Gnifetti	0163 78 01 5
Goûter	04 50 54 40 93
Grands Mulets	04 50 53 16 98
Grands St. Bernards Monastery	0277 4 92 36
Langfluh	0279 57 21 32
Mantova	0163 78 15 0
Margherita	0163 91 03 9
Mezzalama	0125 30 72 26
Monte Rosa	0279 67 21 15
Mont Fort	0277 78 13 84
Prafleuri	0272 81 11 56
Quintino Sella	0125 36 61 13
Saleina	0277 83 17 00
Schönbiel	0279 67 13 54

Täsch	0279 67 39 13
Tête Rousse	04 50 58 24 97
Trient	0277 83 14 38
Valsorey	0277 87 11 22
Velan	0277 87 13 13
Vignettes	0277 83 13 22

Bibliography

Alpine Ski Touing by Jeremy Whitehead (Cordee)

Alpinism, An Introduction to Safe Climbing by Peter Cliff (Cordee)

Avalanche Safety for Skiers and Climbers by Tony Daffern (Cordee)

Mountain Navigation by Peter Cliff (Cordee)

Mt. Blanc Ski de Randonnee by F. Burnier & D. Potard

Ski de Randonnée by Francois Labande (Artou 1989)

Walliser Alpen by Michel Vaucher (Bruckmann 1990)

The Author – Peter Cliff

I am an International Mountain Guide based in Yorkshire (UK) and the Alps; and details of my courses are on my **website www.skisafaris.co.uk**. I hope you find this guidebook helpful and I always welcome feedback, either by email to **peter@skisafaris.co.uk** or by normal mail to **Mosswood Cottage, Crayke, York, YO61 4TQ, England.**

Index